HUGO von HOFMANNSTHAL

In the same series:

(*continued on page* 143)

MODERN LITERATURE MONOGRAPHS

GENERAL EDITOR: Lina Mainiero

HUGO
VON HOFMANNSTHAL

Lowell A. Bangerter

FREDERICK UNGAR PUBLISHING CO.
NEW YORK

Copyright © 1977 by Frederick Ungar Publishing Co., Inc.
Printed in the United States of America
Designed by Anita Duncan

Library of Congress Cataloging in Publication Data

Bangerter, Lowell A 1941–

   Hugo von Hofmannsthal.

   Bibliography: p.
   Includes index.
   1. Hofmannsthal, Hugo Hofmann, Edler von,
1874–1929—Criticism and interpretation.
PT2617.047Z7324   831′.9′12   76–20408
ISBN 0-8044-2028-9

"Über Vergänglichkeit," "Eigene Sprache," "Ghaselen II," "Ein
Prolog," and "Wo ich nahe" from *Gedichte und Lyrische Dramen*
by Hugo von Hofmannsthal, © Bermann-Fischer Verlag AB,
Stockholm, 1946, were translated for this volume by permission of
S. Fischer Verlag, Frankfurt am Main.

Contents

Chronology

1874: Hugo von Hofmannsthal is born in Vienna on February 1.

1884: H. enters the Wiener Akademisches Gymnasium.

1890: Publishes his first poem, "Question," under the pseudonym Loris Melikow. Other poems appear under various pseudonyms.

1891: His first essay appears, as does his first drama, *Yesterday*. He meets Hermann Bahr, Arthur Schnitzler, and other men of letters. Friendship with Stefan George begins.

1892: H. graduates from Gymnasium, begins writing for *Blätter für die Kunst*. He enters law school at the University of Vienna.

1893: Because of friction with George, H. withdraws from contributing to *Blätter für die Kunst*.

1894: He drops out of the university and enters military service.

1895–99: He studies Romance philology and receives doctorate in March 1899.

1901: H. marries Gertrud Schlesinger.

1902: H.'s daughter Christiane is born. He travels to Italy; begins work on *Venice Preserved*. He writes *The Letter of Lord Chandos*.

1903: H. meets Max Reinhardt; writes *Electra*. With it Reinhardt gives H. his first theatrical success. H.'s son Franz is born.

1906: The friendship with Stefan George is terminated.

H. begins productive relationship with Richard Strauss. H.'s son Raimund is born.

1909: The opera version of *Electra* premieres. He begins work on libretto for *Der Rosenkavalier*.

1911: He writes *Everyman*. It premieres in December but receives unfavorable reviews. He writes the libretto for *Ariadne auf Naxos*.

1914–17: H. serves in the military, then in a post of the Austrian War Ministry. He travels extensively on secret political missions.

1917: H. participates in the founding of the Salzburg Festival.

1919: *Die Frau ohne Schatten* premieres in Vienna.

1920: *Everyman* is performed for the first time at the Salzburg Festival and becomes extremely popular. H. completes *The Difficult Man*.

1922: *The Salzburg Great Theater of the World* premieres and meets with popular acclaim.

1924: H. completes *Die ägyptische Helene* and the first version of *The Tower*.

1928: The two versions of *The Tower* premiere simultaneously in Munich and Hamburg. *Die ägyptische Helene* premieres in Dresden.

1929: H. is ill, yet travels a great deal during the early part of the year. On July 13 his son Franz commits suicide. On July 15, H. dies of a cerebral hemorrhage at his home near Vienna.

1

Life Is Loneliness

"There was hardly anyone, great or small, noble or common, who would not have immediately sensed this complete uniqueness and strangeness."[1] In a few words of reminiscence about his friend, the poet, essayist, and critic, Rudolf Borchardt captures the essence of Hugo von Hofmannsthal's impact upon his contemporaries, both as a man and as a poet. Those who knew him best viewed and treated him as a man apart. What irony! There has probably been no other German writer since Goethe who wanted so much to be a part of everything he experienced, and to share with others the entire spectrum of that experience. If Hofmannsthal's life and writings had a single dominant theme, it was that of synthesis, of bringing all things harmoniously together—people, nations, art forms, traditions, ideas, past, present, future. Yet throughout his life he remained an outsider. In a letter of 1912, Hofmannsthal wrote: "I am lonely, as is every man of my nature."[2]

In this context loneliness must not be confused with social isolation. The young Hofmannsthal's home environment precluded such a possibility. Rather, his youth was dominated by such a multitude of complex human relationships that he inevitably learned to meet the demands of a cosmopolitan society at an early age.

Born in Vienna on February 1, 1874, Hugo Laurenz August Hofmann Edler von Hofmannsthal was the only son of a prominent bank director. A mixed heritage, consisting of Austrian, Italian, and German Jewish elements, played an important role in his cultural and intellectual development.

Until age ten he was educated by private tutors. Then, in 1884, he entered the Wiener Akademisches Gymnasium. Because of his social status, his personality, and his obvious intellectual gifts, he was immediately marked by fellow students and teachers alike as somebody out of the ordinary. Edmund von Hellmer remembers his boyhood association with Hofmannsthal in those days in the following terms: "He certainly never became a real schoolboy, although he was by no means a spoilsport and only seldom excluded himself from a game or prank."[3]

While in school Hofmannsthal became an avid reader and assimilated an astonishing wealth of knowledge in a very short time. The Swiss historian Carl J. Burckhardt, who became Hofmannsthal's friend while assigned to the Swiss embassy in Vienna in 1918, remarked that at age sixteen Hofmannsthal had already touched upon every area of intellectual tradition.[4] At school, however, his demonstration of incredibly precocious intellectual achievement served primarily to set him further apart from those around him, and contributed to his ever-increasing feeling of being spiritually alone. Indeed, Hofmannsthal was to remember his school years as the loneliest of his life.

Like every experience he ever had, Hofmannsthal's loneliness was productive. He responded to it with hard work, in which he found a sense of belonging, a feeling which was otherwise missing from his personal life. As he phrased it in a letter to a friend in 1899: "To be sure, when a person works he is not lonely, because he rummages around in the deepest of his memories and really touches on everything that he has ever experienced, yes, even seen and felt, and through work one often unites

with the existences of other people more deeply than
through interaction or reflection."[5] Because of this attitude, Hugo von Hofmannsthal was already on his way to
becoming an established poet by the time he graduated
from the gymnasium in 1892.

Hofmannsthal's literary career began in 1890.
Under the pseudonym Loris Melikow, he published his
first poem, "Question," in the Viennese periodical *An der
schönen blauen Donau*. That same summer he met the
actor Gustav Schwarzkopf. This was an important encounter for the young poet. It was Schwarzkopf who introduced Hofmannsthal to the group of young moderns
that frequented the Café Griensteidl, a popular gathering
place for writers. Among the literary figures he eventually
met there were Hermann Bahr, Arthur Schnitzler, and
Felix Salten. In the ensuing months Hofmannsthal published additional poems in *An der schönen blauen Donau*
and *Die moderne Rundschau*. By late 1891, both his first
literary essay and his first lyric play, *Yesterday*, had appeared in the Berlin publication *Moderne*.

It is not putting it too strongly to say that Hofmannsthal's early creative and critical efforts astounded
the literary community. His particular combination of
youth and virtuosity was an unparalleled phenomenon in
the history of German letters. Many of his contemporaries found it extremely difficult to reconcile the
maturity and evident mastery evinced in his writings
with the teen-aged poet-critic who had written them. The
tenor of Vienna's initial reaction to Hofmannsthal is typi-
fied in the rather humorous account that Hermann Bahr
wrote in 1892, describing his own first meeting with
Hofmannsthal in April, 1891.

Bahr, then already an established writer and critic,
had read a review about his own works written under the
byline "Loris." Extremely impressed by the article, Bahr
was eager to meet its author, whom he pictured as being
"somewhere between forty and fifty, in the maturity of

the intellect—otherwise he could not possess this resigned calmness, . . . apparently belonging to the old
nobility, where beauty, moderation, and dignity are inherited effortlessly, educated by the Jesuits at Kalksburg,
hence the dialectic energy, the logical acrobatics, the
chess-player nature of his understanding."[6] A day or so
after reading the review, Bahr was sitting in the Café
Griensteidl. "A young man with incredible energy" came
up and introduced himself as Loris. Bahr summed up his
reaction in these words: "On that occasion I must have
had the most foolish look on my face that I have ever had
in my life."[7]

Among those most impressed by the young Hofmannsthal's work was the symbolist poet Stefan George.
In December, 1891, George came to Vienna to meet
Hofmannsthal. The two met for the first time at the Café
Griensteidl a few days before Christmas. That encounter
began a productive, if frequently stormy, literary friendship that lasted fifteen years.

Stefan George was a literary elitist. That is, he believed in a literature written by and for a select few.
George hoped that the young Hofmannsthal would share
his point of view, but when Hofmannsthal resisted, tension between the two men began to build. In an undated
letter, which Hofmannsthal received on January 10, 1892,
George lamented that the "meaningful intellectual alli-
ance" that he had anticipated was not really possible
because "each has already arrived at a specific turn of
life, within which he is confined and from which he can
never remove himself."[8] Shortly thereafter George expressed his growing frustration with Hofmannsthal in
terms that make it sound as though they were adver-
saries. "How long shall we continue to play hide-and-
seek? If you want to speak freely (which is now also my
purpose) I invite you to appear again in a neutral
place."[9]

Nevertheless, George remained determined to bring

the young Austrian under his direct influence. Accordingly, in May, 1892, he invited Hofmannsthal to assist in the publication of *Blätter für die Kunst*, a new literary journal that was to feature writings that conformed to George's elitist ideals. The journal was to be put out by George in collaboration with a group of like-minded writers. Hofmannsthal accepted the invitation. As a result, his *Death of Tizian*, a verse play, appeared in the first issue in October, 1892.

Initially, Hofmannsthal was quite comfortable in George's group. In a letter of February 20, 1929, he recalled that early period. "I felt myself to be among my own, without having to take a step away from myself."[10] And yet, as the George-Hofmannsthal correspondence testifies, even then that harmony was extremely tenuous. Because of the marked differences in their temperaments, the two poets frequently had difficulties in communicating. When Hofmannsthal visited George in Vienna and Berlin, he took friends with him in order to avoid having to face George alone. In frustration, George refused to communicate at all, except indirectly through Carl August Klein, a member of George's group who managed the business affairs of *Blätter für die Kunst*.

Hofmannsthal, for his part, developed reservations concerning the value of the periodical. In particular, he felt uncomfortable that his writings were being used to raise the quality of what—except for his own and George's contributions—was a rather lackluster literary enterprise. Hofmannsthal therefore refused to cooperate to the full extent that George and his collaborators expected. Hence, when asked by Klein to write a newspaper article about *Blätter für die Kunst*, Hofmannsthal refused, saying: "It is not very agreeable to me to write an essay about the *Blätter* for a daily newspaper. For my taste, there is in the issues to date: (1) too little that is of real value; (2) too much by me."[11]

By the summer of 1893, the continuing friction had

caused Hofmannsthal to want to divorce himself from
further involvement with the George circle. In a letter of
July 17, he asked George to view his relationship with the
Berlin-based magazine henceforth as that of "an occasional collaborator, and otherwise as a neutral member of
a well-disposed public."[12] George was unwilling to accept those terms. Klein promptly announced in the journal that for personal reasons Hofmannsthal had ended
his active collaboration. Nevertheless, poems and other
writings that Hofmannsthal had already submitted for
publication continued to appear in *Blätter für die Kunst*
in almost every issue until 1897.

Hofmannsthal had met George at the beginning of a
period of social as well as literary growth, a period of
important formative experience. During the 1890s Hofmannsthal traveled extensively, met a broad spectrum of
people, and established the patterns that permanently
characterized his life style.

In 1892, after his graduation from the gymnasium,
he made his first trip to Venice, a city that intrigued him
for the rest of his life. Almost thirty years later, Carl J.
Burckhardt informed Hofmannsthal of his own impending first visit to Venice and characterized Hofmannsthal's
rapport with the city in these words: "I won't write you
from there. That is your city. There you are present, are
again the host and I the guest."[13] Indeed, Venice became
a second home to Hofmannsthal and the setting for some
of his most significant literary works.

In the autumn of 1892, Hofmannsthal enrolled in
law school at the University of Vienna. Law was not his
own choice, but that of his father. Hofmannsthal never
really warmed to his legal studies and consequently
dropped them after only four semesters. He reenrolled at
the university during the winter semester of 1895–96,
this time in Romance philology. Pursuing this course of
study to its conclusion, he received the degree of Doctor
of Philosophy in March, 1899.

After enlisting in 1893, Hofmannsthal began a year of active duty in October, 1894, with the Sixth Dragoon Regiment. A year later he was promoted to sergeant major and transferred to the Eighth Lancer Regiment as a member of the reserves. His final promotion was to reserve lieutenant in 1897. At the end of December, 1905, he resigned his commission, having completed the minimum ten years of reserve service. All in all, the military "adventure" had been a disappointment.

From a literary standpoint, however, the late 1890s were extremely productive for Hofmannsthal. During August and September, 1897, for example, he made a long bicycle trip to Italy, eventually arriving at Varese, where he spent about a month writing. During the first two weeks he wrote more than two thousand lines of poetry and lyric drama! Among the works completed during his flurry of activity was *The Woman in the Window*, which premiered in Berlin on May 5, 1898, and was the first of his theatrical works to be staged. In Italy again during the fall of 1898, he wrote two more plays, *The Marriage of Sobeide* and *The Adventurer and the Singer*, which premiered simultaneously in 1899, on the same program and in both Berlin and Vienna.

In 1901, Hofmannsthal married Gertrud Schlesinger. After a brief honeymoon in Venice, the couple moved to a house in Rodaun, near Vienna. This became their permanent home.

For Hofmannsthal, marriage was a singularly important aspect of life. This fact is evidenced not only by his treatments of its complexities in various literary works, but also in his attitudes toward his own family life. His views on marriage are underscored in the following words from a 1926 letter to Burckhardt: "To me, marriage is something noble, truly the sacrament—I would not like to think of life without marriage."[14]

Nevertheless, his marriage did require a certain amount of personal adjustment. For one thing, Hof-

mannsthal was forced to the realization that he could
not share everything with his wife. In a letter to Burckhardt he wrote, recalling those first years: "When I married Gerty, she was twenty and I was twenty-seven—and
I never thought about whether she was interested in the
conversations that I conduct with my friends. And when
I'd read something aloud, it was not very pleasant for
her and she'd leave the room."[15] Still, the couple was
compatible, and, on the whole, the marriage was a happy
one.

Shortly after the turn of the century, Hofmannsthal
also broke permanently with Stefan George. George had,
by this time, become the most important poet among the
German symbolists. Although Hofmannsthal had been
attempting to withdraw from George's influence since
1893, George had never ceased trying to win the way-
ward Austrian back. Often he had tried to appeal to
Hofmannsthal with open praise, like the following from a
letter of 1897: "In judging your art, I need only repeat,
that aside from some of Paul Gerardy's profound reflections, I know of nothing in our contemporary language
that is as immensely admirable and meaningful."[16]

Hofmannsthal, for his part, had been conciliatory
and had endeavored from his own perspective to make
the friendship fruitful. After all, much of his best early
work had first appeared in *Blätter für die Kunst*, in part
at least as a result of George's encouragement. As late as
May, 1902, he was still able to write: "Be assured that
the passing years have not alienated me from you, rather
they have brought me closer."[17]

Nevertheless, after 1900 it became increasingly obvious that the rapport between them was collapsing. Although Hofmannsthal again published some of his writing in *Blätter für die Kunst* in 1903 and 1904, he and
George seemed to have less and less in common. In a
typical letter of July, 1902, George excused his delay in
responding to a letter from Hofmannsthal. "I hesitated a

long time in answering your last letter. There is hardly a point in it about which I don't feel the exact opposite."[18] And finally, in December, 1905: "I'd have responded with greater composure, had not sadness set in over the fact that there hardly seems to be a single point any longer, where we don't misunderstand one another."[19] A few months later, in March, 1906, the final break occurred.

It is important to note that Hofmannsthal did not sever the relationship because of "misunderstandings," whatever George may have tried to imply about the death of their friendship. On the contrary, Hofmannsthal understood very well what George and his followers expected of him—total subservience.

George regarded himself as the center of the poetic universe. He desired that his associates accept him as their prophet. Accordingly, *Blätter für die Kunst* was published privately so that George could exercise complete control, not only over what it contained and who its contributors were, but even over who received copies of the publication.

In 1899, George became acquainted with Friedrich Gundelfinger, the first man who willingly accepted him as absolute master. (Gundelfinger, under the name Friedrich Gundolf, later became a prominent literary historian.) Subsequently, there developed around George a circle of disciples who followed Gundelfinger's example, accepting George as leader and absolute authority. Hofmannsthal, however, found this situation stifling. He recognized that the only solution was to separate himself from George once and for all.

Hofmannsthal devoted the years immediately following 1900 to gaining a greater degree of mastery of the drama. The lyric poet in Hofmannsthal was now dead, and his important narrative works had all been written by the turn of the century, and so he began adapting and rewriting plays by various dramatists. In this he was by no means limited to sources written in German, since he was fluent in English, Spanish, and French.

In August, 1902, Hofmannsthal began writing *Venice Preserved*. The model for his work was an Elizabethan drama of the same title, which Thomas Otway had written in 1682. Hofmannsthal's five-act tragedy was completed in 1904 and was both staged and published early the next year. But it was soundly criticized in the press.

About six weeks after beginning *Venice Preserved*, Hofmannsthal went to Rome to start work on his adaptation of Calderón's *La vida es sueño*. Hofmannsthal's version of this seventeenth-century Spanish play was never performed and was published only posthumously in 1937. Nevertheless, the dramatic material occupied his attention for more than twenty-five years and was given additional treatment in the various versions of *The Tower*. This latter play was a major dramatic project of the 1920s. It survives in at least three variations and is a major document of Hofmannsthal's despair and resignation during the postwar years. Although the author never completed the drama to his own satisfaction, two of the versions premiered simultaneously in 1928. Neither was successful.

Hofmannsthal's most important work of the first few years of the century was *Electra*, a free rendition of Sophocles's play, which he wrote during the summer and autumn of 1903. In May, Hofmannsthal had met Max Reinhardt, who was then director of the Neues Theater in Berlin. It was probably Reinhardt who provided him with the initial stimulus for writing *Electra*. Be that as it may, his production of the play gave Hofmannsthal his first taste of definite theatrical success. Within four days of its premiere, *Electra* was adopted into the repertories of twenty-two theaters. The association with Reinhardt, which lasted the rest of Hofmannsthal's life, was to become a most important factor in his success as a dramatist.

In a sense Hofmannsthal's entire literary future was determined by that one work. *Electra* brought him together not only with Reinhardt, but also with Richard Strauss, for whose music Hofmannsthal was eventually to provide six librettos. The first of these was *Electra*, which Strauss saw performed as a drama in the 1904–05 season.

Hofmannsthal had already approached Strauss about collaborating on a ballet in 1900, but Strauss had rejected the idea even though he liked the scenario that Hofmannsthal had sent. It was not until 1906 that the two got together again. As they worked together on the opera version of *Electra*, Strauss became increasingly aware of the dramatist's poetic genius. So pleased was he with the rewriting of the dialogue, that he called Hofmannsthal "the born librettist." From his perspective this was "the greatest compliment," since he considered it "much more difficult to write a good operatic text than a fine play."[20] Nor did Strauss overestimate the power that lay in the combination of Hofmannsthal's words and his own music. *Electra* had been a resounding success as a play, but the opera version was so much more successful that the play was no longer produced. Strauss's comments on a performance in Milan reflect the enthusiasm with which the opera was received. He wrote to Hofmannsthal: "I've never heard the opera sung so beautifully. Orchestra very good, success colossal, the biggest takings of the season."[21]

Once *Electra* had whetted his appetite, Strauss began to press Hofmannsthal for new librettos. Initially, Strauss was interested in *Cristina's Trip Home*, a comedy based on Casanova's memoirs. When Hofmannsthal insisted on having it produced first on the dramatic stage, Strauss expressed reluctance to set the play to music.

"My misgivings about having Casanova run first as a comedy are of an artistic nature," he wrote, "in that I am not sure it would be a good thing for me if a comedy that hinges so much on its dénouement as your sketch does were to go stale as a stage play even before the premiere of my opera."[22] Nonetheless, Hofmannsthal felt obliged to give the play to Max Reinhardt. He had promised Reinhardt another comedy, *Sylvia*, for the end of January, 1909, but his work on *Cristina's Trip Home* had precluded his finishing the promised play. Therefore, all he had to offer Reinhardt was the Casanova comedy. As a result, Strauss finally gave up the idea of writing music for *Cristinas Heimreise*.

Through the years of their association, Hofmannsthal and Strauss established a phenomenal working rapport. They had differences of opinion, of course, yet both men developed a sense of constructive give-and-take that lent harmony to their collaboration. Perhaps at no other time was that fact as evident as during the writing of *Der Rosenkavalier*, their second and most successful opera.

Individual letters that Hofmannsthal wrote while working on the text seem to indicate a degree of tension between him and the composer. To say the least, Strauss was extremely demanding of his librettist, and it was sometimes difficult for Hofmannsthal to reconcile the composer's recommendations with his own ideas of what the work should become. Occasionally he found himself unable to agree with Strauss at all. Yet his positive attitude in dealing with Strauss's objections successfully ironed out the problems. This is illustrated in the following passage from a letter of July 18, 1909:

Your second letter of the 10th from Mürren contains a remark critical of the dialogue at Lerchenau's entrance and his courtship of Sophie, which, frankly, I do consider unjustified. But I would rather not enlarge on this matter just now, since to do so might endanger the mood of good will and sanguine expectation with which I am embarking upon this revision.[23]

As he wrote *Der Rosenkavalier*, however, Hofmannsthal grew to expect encouragement and active support from Strauss. He later remembered the composer's favorable reaction to each act of the new libretto as "one of the most significant pleasures connected with that work."[24] But so strong was his need for moral support from his collaborator that on one occasion he broke Strauss's prolonged silence with an agitated "What is the matter with you? I get quite anxious when I do not hear from my alter ego for such a long time."[25]

Because Hofmannsthal felt that he and Strauss were kindred spirits, he was openly disappointed when Strauss greeted the finished libretto of *Ariadne auf Naxos* with less enthusiasm than he had shown for *Der Rosenkavalier*. Strauss, for his part, was at first unable to appreciate the internal subtleties of the text. Even after the writer explained them to his satisfaction, Strauss remained skeptical, feeling that a complicated libretto was dangerous. If he had initially found the text difficult, the audience and critics would understand it even less.

It was some time before Strauss warmed to the piece at all. Gradually, however, as he felt his way into it, he found he could create music that enabled the work to achieve in part the internal harmony between words and score that Hofmannsthal had envisioned. Ultimately, *Ariadne auf Naxos* became almost as popular with opera goers as *Der Rosenkavalier*. Nevertheless, Strauss never did match Hofmannsthal's fondness for this particular work.

To some extent Strauss's continued uneasiness about *Ariadne auf Naxos* was probably due to a mistake that Hofmannsthal had made. The latter had originally planned the work as a sort of epilogue to *The Bourgeois as Nobleman*, his adaptation of a comedy by Molière.

From the beginning it was an unhappy juxtaposition. Even Hofmannsthal was later forced to admit that *The Bourgeois as Nobleman* was a failure on the stage. That fact and its unfortunate relationship to the history of *Ariadne auf Naxos* undoubtedly left Strauss with a slightly bitter taste in his mouth.

In May, 1912, Hofmannsthal made one of many trips to Paris. While there, he was strongly impressed by performances of the Russian ballet. Once again he decided to attempt a ballet scenario. Together with Count Harry Kessler, vice-president of the German Artists' Union, he wrote *Legend of Joseph*, based on the experiences of the Old Testament Joseph in the house of Potiphar. He then offered the text to Strauss for composition of the score. It was not until December, 1913, however, that Strauss finally played parts of the music for him. The ballet premiered in May, 1914, just prior to the outbreak of World War I. Hofmannsthal and Strauss journeyed to Paris for the event and enjoyed a major triumph. In June the ballet was equally well received in London.

As World War I approached, Hofmannsthal grew melancholy, realizing that the old Austria, the life style and civilization that he loved, was destined to collapse. In a sense, much of his effort from 1912 on, both political and artistic, was a grand endeavor to preserve as much as possible of that dying culture.

As an officer in the reserve Hofmannsthal was recalled to the army in July, 1914. He served in the war ministry, and during the next two years traveled widely on secret political missions. He wrote patriotic articles and made speeches to groups of Austrian officers. When the Hapsburg monarchy fell, Hofmannsthal was not unprepared for it. Nonetheless, he viewed the death of the old regime as a personal disaster, the loss of an important part of his own life. It was a loss from which he did not fully recover.

In 1913 Hofmannsthal had begun working on the libretto for *Die Frau ohne Schatten*. He had great hopes for the opera and expressed the view in one letter that it would establish him once and for all as Strauss's personal, private poet.[26] The project was nevertheless frustrating, and Hofmannsthal struggled with it throughout the war years. Strauss, who deplored the interruption of his work through the war, prodded Hofmannsthal incessantly for the text. Hofmannsthal, on the other hand, refused to be rushed. In 1913, relatively early in his labors, he had written: "Don't, I implore you, get impatient for *Die Frau ohne Schatten* at this moment—and don't let your wife do so!—or else you will jeopardize not only my nerves but, above all, the work itself. It is a terribly delicate, immensely difficult task and more than once have I been in profound despair."[27] The material occupied much of his attention until the premiere in 1919, at which time he also completed a prose version of the story.

The finished opera was much less popular than the earlier cooperative ventures with Strauss had been. For one thing, Strauss had not been able to fit his music to the mood of the libretto as well as he had in previous efforts. At the same time, audience and critics alike found Hofmannsthal's text difficult to comprehend because of its literary complexities.

At the end of the war Hofmannsthal's interest in the revitalization of the Austrian artistic tradition increased a great deal. He wanted to develop a permanent institution for the purpose of furthering the performing arts and all his hopes for a formal program of cultural rejuvenation were brought to fruition in the Salzburg Festival. Although Hofmannsthal did not initiate the festival, he was surely a most avid supporter.

The Salzburg Festival Theater Corporation was formed in the fall of 1917. In September, 1918, it was decided to form a council to advise in the building of the

theater and the planning of the annual program. Hofmannsthal became a member of that council, joining Max
Reinhardt, Richard Strauss, and others. While serving in
this capacity he gave the festival the program concept
that still governs the annual productions.

The Salzburg area had always been dear to Hofmannsthal. For him it was "the heart of the heart of
Europe."[28] For years he had lived and worked near
Salzburg during the autumn months, his most creative
season of the year. When asked why the festival should
be established there, Hofmannsthal wrote: "Everything
that lives on the German stage has its roots here, both the
poetic element and the theatrical."[29] It was this consciousness of Salzburg's concentration of culture and history that caused Hofmannsthal to support the festival
actively until his death. Not even the Nazis, who boy-
cotted his books and destroyed his statue in Salzburg in
1938, for various reasons including his Jewish ancestry,
his Jewish wife, and his strong Austrian nationalism,
could erase the mark that Hofmannsthal left at Salzburg.

It is significant that Hofmannsthal's most successful
opera and several of his other works were strongly col-
ored by his Austrian background. Frederick Ritter, in his
book on Hofmannsthal and Austria, maintains that the
concept of the creative individual's ties to his homeland is
basic to Hofmannsthal's thought.[30] An obvious illustration of this point is *The Salzburg Great Theater of the
World*, a play that Hofmannsthal wrote especially for the
Salzburg Festival in 1922. Although based on elements
from a seventeenth-century Spanish play, Calderón's *El
gran teatro del mundo*, *The Salzburg Great Theater of
the World* is heavy with the flavor, the atmosphere, the
pomp and pageantry of traditional Austrian Catholicism.
Like *Everyman*, Hofmannsthal's 1911 version of the old
English morality play, *The Salzburg Great Theater of the
World* was extremely successful with the Salzburg public,

even though some critics were less generous with their praise

Life was not easy for Hofmannsthal in the postwar years. In 1919, he found himself a victim of the economic woes that beset his unhappy homeland. In order to meet his financial needs, he was forced to sell his favorite works of art. By 1922 things had got worse. Hofmannsthal feverishly engaged himself in a number of activities designed to improve his financial situation. It was at this time that he began his association with the Bremer Press and its director, Dr. Willy Wiegand.

Partly for economic reasons, and partly because he desired to make German cultural heritage more accessible, Hofmannsthal allowed Wiegand to recruit him for a series of commercial publishing ventures. In 1912 he had edited an anthology of narrative prose entitled *German Storytellers*. He now became involved in several similar undertakings. The first of these was *Das deutsche Lesebuch* (The German Reader) in two volumes, published in 1922 and 1923. Hofmannsthal's financial situation was so precarious that in November, 1922, he wrote Wiegand:

Actually I have gotten into an almost impossible situation here, due to the current relationship between income and the most modest personal expenses. The following, taken purely as an example, will give you a picture: if, in the shortest time, 5,000 copies of each volume of the *Reader* could be sold, then my share would keep me and my household above water for a period of from six to eight weeks.[31]

The German Reader was followed in May, 1923, by *German Epigrams*, a slender book including nine major authors. A third compilation, *Wert und Ehre deutscher Sprache* (Worth and Honor of the German Language), was published in 1927. This work was an anthology of significant comments on the German language by representative cultural figures. It appeared simultaneously with still another book, *Schiller's Self-Characterization*, a revision of a nineteenth-century collection of excerpts from Friedrich Schiller's letters and other writings.

Hofmannsthal would likely have participated in at least some of these projects even without the stimulus of financial need. Taken as a whole, they offered an additional opportunity to refocus public attention on German literary achievements. This was extremely important to Hofmannsthal because he viewed that heritage as an ingrained part of his own personal existence. As Carl J. Burckhardt phrased it: "In the later years of his short life, Hofmannsthal possessed the ability to experience past ages, not from outside, but rather from within the world of their sensations and their ethos."[32]

After the war ended, it was quite a while before Hofmannsthal began a new project for Strauss. He was not satisfied with the way the operas were being handled on the stage, especially in Berlin. In January, 1919, in an outpouring of despair, he virtually threatened to go on strike.

But when I am faced with ugliness as in the case of the décor of all our productions in Berlin, and when these disagreeable sensations impress themselves on the eye, my most sensitive spot, when they recur again and again and become to me a sort of symbol for the prostitution of the child of my imagination in sordid, vulgar "business," then this exasperates me, and this exasperation might for a long period or even permanently incapacitate me for this kind of work.[33]

Finally, however, in 1923 Hofmannsthal began two projects intended to renew the close collaboration with Strauss. The first was a proposed film version of *Der Rosenkavalier*. The details were eventually worked out in 1925. Hofmannsthal tried to involve Strauss in directing the opera for the film production, but to his dismay, Strauss refused. Apparently the latter did not share Hofmannsthal's optimism that the film would be "a positive fillip and new impetus to the opera's success in the theater."[34]

In any case, Strauss was far more interested in the second project. In September, 1923, Hofmannsthal had begun concentrated work on the libretto for *Helen in Egypt*, their fifth opera. He worked on the text off and on for three years. At last, in March, 1926, Strauss was able to play for him the music of the first act, although Strauss took another two years to complete the rest of the score. *Helen in Egypt* was not premiered until 1928, but, as had been the case with *Ariadne auf Naxos*, Hofmannsthal was delighted with the results. He praised the music as more pleasing than any Strauss had written before.

Unfortunately, from the textual standpoint, *Helen in Egypt* was also by far the most complicated of Hofmannsthal's librettos. Both poet and composer were therefore apprehensive about the reception of the opera among critics and public. Their fears were realized. *Helen in Egypt* was even less successful than *The Woman without a Shadow* had been almost a decade earlier. Although the two operas are still performed occasionally, they remain, on the German stage at least, among the least frequently produced of all Hofmannsthal's theatrical works.[35]

Hofmannsthal's final libretto for Strauss was *Arabella*, an opera that he never saw performed. He sent the first act to Strauss in May, 1928. Strauss responded that he found "the characters excellent, and the exposition thrilling and promising," and desired only that the act be pulled more firmly together to facilitate the musical treatment of the individual aspects.[36] By January, 1929, the text was essentially completed to the satisfaction of both men. Hofmannsthal spent the last few months of his life polishing *Arabella*, and Strauss's final communication to him was one of thanks for an outstanding first act. Hofmannsthal, however, never read the telegram, which arrived the day of his death.

This last opera, which was premiered four years after Hofmannsthal died, ended the artistic collaboration of twenty-three years on a very happy note. Unlike the two preceding pieces, *Arabella* enjoyed a success with the public like that of *Der Rosenkavalier*. Indeed, the two operas justify the tribute Strauss had paid Hofmannsthal on the latter's fiftieth birthday: "It was your words which drew from me the finest music that I had to give."[37]

As a young man Hofmannsthal had taken refuge from his loneliness in his work and so sought oneness with the world. His whole life was a continuous intensification of that pursuit. Thus, in spite of his disillusionment at the end of the war, his last years were extremely active ones. It was almost as though he knew how short his time was. Engaged in a multitude of literary projects, he traveled more than ever before. Italy, Sicily, Switzerland, France, and England were his frequent destinations during the 1920s. In 1925 he went to North Africa and was so impressed that he was reluctant to return to Europe. He also encouraged his three children, especially his sons, to travel.

Unfortunately, Hofmannsthal's health prevented many of the things that he wanted to do. He suffered from two chronic ailments, high blood pressure and a sensitivity to the weather, which often rendered him unable to work.

Beginning with a long siege of illness early in 1920, Hofmannsthal was recurrently ill for the rest of his life.

Hofmannsthal's last days were tragic ones, more tragic at least than he was able spiritually and physically to endure. On July 13, 1929, his older son, Franz, committed suicide in his parents' home.

Two days later, as Hofmannsthal prepared to leave for his son's funeral, he suffered a massive cerebral hemorrhage. One of Austria's greatest writers of the twentieth century was dead. He joined his unfortunate son in a common grave.

2

The Theory of Life

In 1891 Hofmannsthal published an essay entitled "On the Physiology of Modern Love." That firstling begins as follows: "Paul Bourget's artistic development is not a progression from problem to problem; rather it is an increase in depth in the comprehension of a phenomenon." Had the subject been his own progress, rather than that of his French contemporary, Hofmannsthal might well have made the same observation. To him, life was *the* great wonder. By shaping its sundry aspects into literary works, he hoped better to understand his special internal world. The most important goal of his writing was the explanation and the education of the self. Nowhere is that more evident than in his essays.

The essay is the one literary form that Hofmannsthal cultivated consistently throughout his life. Altogether he wrote more than two hundred essays. The spectrum of topics is astounding; they range from Beethoven to Eugene O'Neill, from Czechoslovakia to Africa, from classical antiquity to Buddhism. Yet each subject receives such careful attention that each essay reads as if the matter at hand were Hofmannsthal's only concern.

The essays also vary considerably in form. Some of them are even written as dialogues, others as letters. For each essay, Hofmannsthal chose a style suited and masterfully adapted to the content. Most of them are rich in the imagery that he considered essential to great literature. They do not simply communicate or inform; they are artistic masterpieces, products of the creative imagination rather than the analytical intellect. Their language is often poetic, even rhythmic, full of color and nuance.

"Poesy and Life," first published in 1896, is characteristic of Hofmannsthal's early essays in both tone and direction. The subject of the essay is the literary criticism of the time, the validity of which Hofmannsthal openly challenged on the grounds that it was too superficial. His intent was to motivate a change in the way that both reviewers and public looked at writers and their art. He insisted that they penetrate beyond incidentals in their evaluations.

According to Hofmannsthal, the major defect in modern literary criticism was the tendency to dissect a given work into a panorama of component parts. By dwelling on individual aspects and relating specific details of the works to elements in the real world of the writer, critics were losing sight of the meaning of the work as a whole. In "Poesy and Life," Hofmannsthal explicitly contrasted his own approach to literature with that of the "philologists, journalists, and pseudopoets" as follows: "Their praise is directed toward fragments and parts, mine toward the whole; their appreciation toward the relative, mine toward the absolute."

It should be said that the above quotation is important beyond its contribution to this particular essay. In it lies the quintessence of Hofmannsthal's critical approach not only to literature, but also to life itself. In a very real sense, each of his essays, no matter what the topic, reveals Hofmannsthal's concern for the whole, the composite, the synthesis. For that reason, in her exhaustive study of the essays, Elsbeth Pulver concluded that they reveal above all "the writer's unceasing effort to grasp the phenomena to which he addresses himself—individual works, literary figures, complete eras, even national literatures—in their living entirety."[1]

"Poesy and Life" is especially significant in that its focus is the concept of wholeness as it pertains to literature vis-à-vis the real world. In antithesis to the German realists of the second half of the nineteenth century and the naturalists of the 1890s, Hofmannsthal declared that reality is not a necessary part of literature. Moreover, he argued that a work of literature, as an independent whole, valid in itself, must be regarded as separate from life. In the essay he phrased it this way: "No direct path leads from poesy to life, nor does any lead from life to poesy." The strength of literature, as Hofmannsthal presented it here, should be its ability to symbolize, rather than to imitate, life. Even the act of creating the poetic work symbolizes the individual's relationship to his own identity. That is, through the process of putting together the elements of his existence, the individual actually creates his identity, much as the writer forms a poem from the raw material.

In a way, "Poesy and Life" is an elegy on modern man's lack of understanding of what literature really is. A work of literature, for Hofmannsthal, is a symbol. It consists of a unique ordering of words and ideas rather than a composite of elements drawn from life and its experiences. In the essay, he even went so far as to say that "the words are everything." Language, not experience, is the raw material of literature; and it is the new language construct, a symbol formed from previously existing elements, that can affect life.

Hofmannsthal concluded that both the literature and the literary criticism of his own time were failing because neither poet nor critic understood the true nature of literature. The poet had apparently lost the ability to employ the language to create a symbolic whole. The concept of wholeness itself, which existed in earlier eras, had been lost. As a result, both poets and nonpoets appeared incapable of more than a fragmentary relationship to existence, to their own identities, and to literary art.

Despite his intense personal involvement with the ideas he introduced in "Poesy and Life," Hofmannsthal remained informal, almost casual, in their presentation. The form is that of a lecture, but the style is chatty. Occasional witticisms make the essay less formidable, and the arguments are couched in gently persuasive language. The result is an extremely readable piece of prose.

In 1902, Hofmannsthal published a much more elaborate and subjective discussion of wholeness as it pertains to the poet and his art. The work, entitled simply "A Letter," appeared in the Berlin daily newspaper *Der Tag*, and became Hofmannsthal's most famous essay.

The opening lines identify it as a letter written by Phillip Lord Chandos (an imaginary person) to Sir Francis Bacon, the famous seventeenth-century English scientist and philosopher. Chandos is a one-time poet who has ceased to write. In response to an inquiry from Bacon, he tries to explain why he has abandoned all literary activity. Chandos addresses not Bacon the scientist-statesman-philosopher, but Bacon the essayist, the master of language and expression. Hofmannsthal apparently felt that Bacon would have understood the plight of the poet who had lost both the facility to express himself coherently and altogether the ability to cope with language.

In the letter Chandos recalls his years as a young writer. At age nineteen he had written pastoral plays on themes from Greek myth. By age twenty-three he had progressed to expressing himself in Latin. In other words, he had been a rather typical product of Renaissance humanism. As a poet he had had great plans. Among them was a major literary work on the early reign of Henry VIII. Legends and fables had also attracted him, and he had desired to interpret them, seeing them as storehouses of secrets that should be revealed. Like Julius Caesar, as described by Cicero, Chandos had intended to compile a collection of apothegms: noteworthy quotations from his contemporaries and the ancients;

notes on special experiences and events; descriptions of impressive works of architecture and other wonders. Suddenly, however, two years prior to his writing the letter, he had given up all thought of a literary career.

Now, at age twenty-six, Chandos contrasts his current condition with that of those earlier years. All his literary activities had been based on a specific view of existence. He had seen everything as a great unity. Nature had been a part of each phenomenon, and he in turn had felt himself present in all aspects of nature. Yet two years earlier this sense of harmony had ceased. Lost was the power to synthesize, to see things as a whole. In his own words: "My situation, in short, is this: I have completely lost the ability to think or speak about anything at all with continuity."

Chandos attributes his present state to a gradual mental-spiritual breakdown. First he was unable to discuss general topics because he was loath to use abstract terms such as "spirit" and "soul." Then he could no longer formulate opinions about major happenings around him because he had lost the facility of making the necessary abstractions. This psychological malady intensified until it affected the way in which he dealt with even the most trivial, everyday things.

The cause of Chandos's breakdown was the collapse of his rapport with language. His intellect forced him to examine assertions and descriptions in minute detail. Under scrutiny they fell apart. Fragments dissolved into components, which likewise disintegrated, until he could describe nothing for lack of understandable concepts. Words themselves became empty and meaningless.

Unable to communicate in a meaningful fashion, Chandos lost contact with both the world and his own identity. He was no longer able to apprehend at even a minimal level individual objects, phenomena, and especially himself. In analyzing Chandos's condition, the great Austrian writer Hermann Broch wrote: "The

mystic intuitive unity of self, expression, and thing has
been lost to him in a single blow, so that his ego is
brought to the most hermetic isolation, isolated from a
rich world to which he no longer has access, a world
where the things will no longer communicate to him, not
even their names."[2]

At the time of the letter, Chandos has not recovered
from the breakdown. He is leading a lonely, "spiritless,"
"thoughtless" existence, renovating a wing of his house,
managing his estates, riding through the countryside.
There is a barrier between him and those who surround
him because the latter have no inkling of what is going on
within him. Nevertheless, his situation is not completely
hopeless. There are signs that a transformation is beginning to take place. His experiences force him to look at
his relationship to the world in a new way. The suggestion is that in contrast with his previous interpretation of
reality, in which he saw himself as an omnipresent part of
a great whole, he moves toward a view of the world in
which all external elements are a part of himself. Thus it
is he who becomes the unifying principle.

As yet Chandos has no control over that change in
outlook. He describes its manifestations as occasional
happy and invigorating moments that spontaneously and
unexpectedly burst upon him in "an overwhelming flood
of higher life." He feels unable to convey specifics ade-
quately, however, because human language is unsuited to
the task. His "joyful moments" can perhaps best be characterized as internal experiences stimulated by external
impressions. He enumerates various distinct items that
give rise to these personal "revelations": a dog in the
sun, a lonely churchyard, a small farmhouse, a watering
can. Even chance reflections on things not immediately
present serve at times to generate new and unique experiences within him.

One example of such a mystical event is especially
vivid. Chandos tells about having given an order to

poison the rats in the milk cellars of his dairy. As he takes an evening ride through the fields, a vision of the dying rats assaults his mind. His phrasing is interesting: "Suddenly that cellar opened up within me, filled with the death struggle of that nation of rats. Everything was inside me." The result of such occurrences is a feeling of actual physical involvement with other realms of existence. Each thing encountered is a world in itself, and Chandos sees his own body as the key that can open those worlds.

Yet when the spell ends and the door to his inner universe is closed, Chandos can describe neither the nature of the harmony that momentarily existed, nor the way in which a sense of that harmony conveyed itself to him. This fact causes him to finish his letter by concluding that he will probably never write again. After all, the only language that could really capture his internal world is one of feeling, a language of which he claims to know not a single word.

By Hofmannsthal's own admission, "A Letter" is related to events from his own life. On the basis of comments from his correspondence as well as other evidence, scholars have developed a standardized explanation of that relationship. The accepted view has been recapitulated by the critic Donald G. Daviau as follows: "After a richly productive decade as a lyric poet and lyric dramatist, Hofmannsthal experienced a crisis in his productivity around 1900, which caused him to renounce the writing of poetry in order to devote himself to the new goal of achieving more popular success in the theater."[3]

Be that as it may, it is interesting that, according to Hofmannsthal, the initial stimulus for the Chandos letter came not from his crisis, but rather from Francis Bacon's essays. In a letter to Leopold von Andrian, dated January 16, 1903, Hofmannsthal illuminated the genesis of "A Letter" as follows:

In August I often leafed through the essays of Bacon. I found the closely personal nature of this era attractive, and dreamed myself into the way in which these people of the sixteenth century perceived antiquity. I then had the desire to create something in this literary tone. The content, which I had to borrow from a personal inner event, a living experience, in order not to have a cold effect, simply added itself.[4]

It is not clear what drew Hofmannsthal specifically to Bacon in the first place, but his general interest in the Elizabethan period was strong at the time (August 1902) because he was just beginning his adaptation of an Elizabethan tragedy, Thomas Otway's *Venice Preserved*.

Perhaps the most peculiar thing about the Chandos letter is its inherent paradox. While the fictitious author claims to be unable to employ language effectively, the essay itself is a masterpiece of literary artistry. The images are bright, colorful, and vibrant. The selection of words and the organization of ideas are flawless. Each sentence, each phrase is constructed with care and precision, is impregnated with life and meaning. The whole is ordered so as to allow each detail to convey its message with power. In short, it is not the work of a spiritually disturbed Chandos, but of the virtuoso Hofmannsthal. This combination of his flawless style and his deep insights into the specific problems of literary creativity and effective use of the language have made "A Letter" a landmark of the modern European essay.

Both "Poesy and Life" and "A Letter" are representative of Hofmannsthal's essays as a whole, in that to a greater or lesser degree they describe how he conceived of his own relationship to the world around him. Yet they differ from many of his essays in that they treat broad, general problems. Most of Hofmannsthal's other essays are less theoretical. They are, generally, investigations into the specific yet varied phenomena that he personally encountered. One may take the position that the essays are a concerted attempt to define life itself in terms of its individual manifestations.

As a group, the essays can be readily subdivided into several categories. By far the largest of these comprises those essays that deal with literature. Yet other important categories are studies on art, music, and the theater; writings on history and politics; and essays giving impressions of places that he visited.

The essays on literature are significant for the depth and sensitivity with which Hofmannsthal treated a broad range of literary topics. In addition, they are cosmopolitan in every sense. Besides treating writers and literary creations from England, France, Italy, Russia, and America, as well as Germany, Austria, and Switzerland, the essays are addressed to varying publics. Among the most interesting, for example, are five "Vienna Letters" that were written during the early 1920s for the *Dial*, a New York literary review. (The *Dial* was noted for presenting the work of both avant-garde writers and distinguished scholars.)

In those letters, Hofmannsthal attempted to give the readers of the *Dial* a feeling for contemporary Austrian literary currents. A passage from the fifth letter to the *Dial*, in its original version, illustrates Hofmannsthal's enthusiasm for what was happening in Austrian literature. In the context of a discussion of the Austrian peasant poet Richard Billinger, Hofmannsthal wrote:

If the gift for art which is stored up in all these lonely valleys seizes on the mysterious inner meaning of things—instead of unburdening itself through the hand, by the brush or the woodcutter's knife—then a poet results, while his talent usually remains in the sphere of dialect, which is close to the soil and is, we might say, still accessible to its nightly resuscitation, its dew. For with us Europeans dialect is by no means the speech of the upper classes in a state of shoddy and unbeautiful corruption, but it is the code of primitive natural sounds whence the speech of the intellectuals is continually drawing new life. But in this case, in the case of this young and astonishing peasant poet, Richard Billinger, it is written German, the high language of literature, in which, with the sureness of genius, things are spoken and images evoked that belong completely to these relatively childish peasant subjects.

Most important, the essays on literature contribute to an understanding of Hofmannsthal's own development as a writer. Among other things, they illuminate his rapport with literary precursors and contemporaries and document in detail the debt he owed to the others. An excellent example is found in one of three short tributes to Schiller published in 1905. Hofmannsthal wrote: "I believe that at no time in my life, from my fifteenth year on, have I ever lost contact with Schiller and his writings." And in the same piece: "The Goethe-Schiller correspondence belongs among those books that I would find most difficult to do without if I had to choose a small number from among all the books in existence." Intensive scholarly investigations have confirmed the tremendous influence that both Schiller and Goethe had on him.[5]

The essays on art, music, and theater, like everything he wrote, reveal a great deal about Hofmannsthal. More than anything else, they testify to an intense and lasting commitment to European cultural heritage. Hofmannsthal felt strongly that interest in traditional art forms should not die out in a materialistic age. He therefore employed his writing skills at every opportunity to encourage cultural activity and to increase public awareness of what was taking place in the arts. He tried to increase the visibility of artists, composers, performers, and cultural institutions by devoting essays and series of essays to their activities.

Nor were those endeavors unsuccessful. Hofmannsthal had the power to make the personalities, the works of art, the institutions that he loved, come alive so that they could never be forgotten by those who read what he had written. To find ample confirmation of that fact, one need only read his essays on Eleonora Duse, the great Italian-born actress. Perhaps no greater tribute has ever been paid any actress than that paid when he wrote of Duse: "She plays, quite simply, everything: life in its living entirety."

Like those of other groups, Hofmannsthal's historical and political essays are diverse as to subject matter. Nevertheless, one theme dominated over the others: Austria and the sociopolitical order in which the author grew up. Hofmannsthal was nothing if not a patriot.

In 1915, he wrote his most famous political-historical essay, *Prinz Eugen, der edle Ritter* (Prince Eugene, the Noble Knight). His express purpose in writing it was to help instill in the rising generation a "love of the fatherland." In twelve segments he portrayed the career of Eugene of Savoy (1663–1736), an Austrian general, born in France, whom Hofmannsthal regarded as *the* great Austrian. Eugene first fought in 1683 during the Turkish siege of Vienna. He later led Austrian armies for thirty-nine years, and won his most famous victory during the Battle of Belgrade. The flavor of Hofmannsthal's essay is captured in the title of the poem that forms the final section: "Prince Eugene's spirit is always there, where our soldiers fight and win."

Among the very best of Hofmannsthal's essays are those that convey his impressions of places he visited. His descriptions of scenes along the wayside have a beauty unexcelled in German letters. A good example appears in the opening paragraph of an essay describing his visit to a thousand-year-old monastery near Mount Parnassus in central Greece. Entitled "The Monastery of Saint Luke," the essay was written in 1908 and forms the first portion of a larger work, *Moments in Greece*. It reads in part:

Many stretches were bleak with the solitude of millennia, with nothing more than a lizard rustling across the path and a hawk circling in the air high above. . . . Then the wolflike dogs, barking and showing their teeth, came near to the mules; and they had to be driven back with stones. Sheep, heavy with wool, stood pressed together in the shade of a block of stone, shaken by their own heated breathing. Two black rams butted each other with their horns. A handsome young shepherd carried a small lamb on his shoulders.

In his essays, as in everything else he wrote, Hofmannsthal combined the elements of his experience into verbal portraits, into a unique world, a world that mirrored parts of what was inside himself. Each of his essays can be made to yield up such a part of him, and these parts in turn form a new whole, a picture of the universe that the essayist discovered outside and recreated within himself.

3

The Search for Identity

Hofmannsthal's first attempt at narrative prose yielded
something quite different from what he had initially anticipated. In a letter of 1892 to a friend he had declared
his intent to write "a fairytale, golden brown and
orange,"[1] from the tales of the Arabian Nights. Yet the
promised warmth and color never materialized. Instead,
the *Tale of the Merchant's Son and His Servants* proved
to be a rather cold, uncomfortable, though highly pol-
ished and poetic story. Hofmannsthal's friend, the Austrian writer Arthur Schnitzler, accurately described the
work in a letter he wrote to Hofmannsthal on November
26, 1895: "The story has nothing of the warmth and
glow of a fairytale, yet in a wonderful manner it does
have the pale light of the dream, of its puzzling and hazy
transitions, and the peculiar mixture of clarity of the
minor things and the fadedness of the special things, that
belong to the dream."[2]

Despite the implications of the work's title—the
literal translation of which is The Fairytale of the
672nd Night—the tale bears no resemblance to the tale
of the 672nd Arabian Night. As Wolfgang Köhler has
pointed out in an extensive study of the work, Hofmannsthal at most borrowed a minor episode from one of the
Arabian Nights tales and built his own narrative around
it.[3]

The *Tale of the Merchant's Son and His Servants*

concerns a young man who tries to withdraw from society, and in so doing ultimately causes his own destruction. The protagonist, who is never identified by name, leaves his meaningless existence in the city and retires to a country estate with four servants. In the country, his dealings with the servants remain equally meaningless until he receives a letter that accuses his valet of vile misdeeds. The merchant's son suddenly realizes that the servants' lives are a part of his own life and therefore views the letter as a threat to his existence. He returns to the city to straighten out the matter, but arrives too late in the day to accomplish anything immediately. In a poorer section of town he enters a small jewelry shop and buys gifts for his housekeeper and one of the maids.

Then, out of curiosity, he visits a nearby greenhouse, in which a child, who reminds him of the other maid, locks him in. After escaping through a small door and, on a narrow board over a chasm between two buildings, he returns to the street. While making his way back to the more prosperous section of town in search of lodgings for the night, he comes close to military barracks. In front of the barracks a horse kicks him in the stomach. He is carried by soldiers to an empty room, where he dies cursing his servants for having caused his death.

In a manner reminiscent of his contemporary Franz Kafka, Hofmannsthal presents the fate of the merchant's son as a kind of horror story. The protagonist is forced to face a reality from which he cannot escape. His inability to cope with this world leads to his destruction.

Psychologically, it is a real-life situation. Schnitzler, in commenting further on the dreamlike nature of the story, wrote: "There are such dreams, they are actually also destinies, and one could understand that people who are plagued by such dreams kill themselves in despair."[4]

The merchant's son gets into trouble because he denies his own identity. He wants to be merely a spectator in a universe that demands that he act. In Hofmannsthal's framework, where individual and world form an inseparable unit, the kind of withdrawal from society that the merchant's son attempts is really a retreat from the self.

It is important to note that the merchant's son does not back off from social involvement ignorantly. However incompletely, he is aware of his interdependency with what surrounds him. Life in the city has taught him that his personal realm is a microcosm of existence. "All the forms and colors of the world" live in the furnishings of his house, and his home is "an enchanted picture of the interlaced wonders of the world." Nevertheless, he does not regard these relationships as important. Indeed, by dwelling on "the nothingness of all these things," he becomes aware of the vanity of his own life and subconsciously longs for death.

The move to the country can therefore be interpreted as an act of free will directed toward the realization of the subconscious death wish. This idea is implied when the merchant's son tells himself: "Your feet carry you to where you are to die."

Once alone in the country with his servants, however, the young man cannot avoid thinking about his relationship to them. More important, he feels them watching him, feels them live "more strongly, more intensely than he feels himself live." He gradually comes to view the servants as extensions of himself, who are as conscious of what goes on within him as he is. The result is fear and the unavoidable confrontation with self, for him a most unpleasant experience. To use the words of the story: "More terrible than the fact that they unceasingly observed him was that they forced him . . . to think about himself."

Unfortunately, the merchant's son remains unwilling to come to grips with the problem of his identity. Despite his awareness that the servants are a part of him, he tries to ignore them. Finally, however—and this is the crucial point—circumstances compel him to acknowledge his responsibility to them.

The anonymous letter that accuses the valet and threatens to expose him transforms a simple matter of personal duty into a struggle for self-preservation. Briefly at least, the instinct for survival seems to dominate over the death wish as the merchant's son becomes conscious of what is really at stake. Hofmannsthal describes the turmoil within him as follows:

The more he thought about it, the more upset he became and the less he could endure the idea of losing one of these beings, with whom he had completely coalesced through habit and other mysterious forces. . . . To him it was as though someone had insulted and threatened his most intimate possession and intended to force him to flee from himself and deny that which he loved. . . . He saw his four servants torn from his house, and it seemed to him as though the entire content of his life was departing from him.

Like it or not, the merchant's son no longer has a choice. In order to save his servant, he must return to the society he fled. Unfortunately, his panicky, yet half-hearted action has been too long in coming. Symbolically, he arrives in the city too late in the day to accomplish his purpose.

When the merchant's son wanders into the dingy, rundown section of town, it is full of impressions and people that remind him of his servants. These reinforce his feelings of guilt and in a sense bear witness against him. It is more to pacify his conscience than anything else that he stops at the jeweler's to buy presents. And, for the same reason, in the greenhouse he offers coins to the little girl whose face reminds him of the younger maid. She, of course, rejects the gift. More important, she passes judgment on him by shutting him in the greenhouse, thus signaling his complete isolation and final separation from the world of his servants. When he escapes, the plank across the chasm does not really free him from his isolation but simply leads him away from his old existence. Since survival in isolation is impossible, his early death is now inevitable.

The peculiar ending of the story has been given various interpretations. Jakob Laubach maintains that the death of the merchant's son is one of sacrifice for the servants.[5] There is no suggestion, however, that the servants themselves benefit from his death in any way. On the other hand, there is ample evidence that his death is in retribution for guilt incurred in what Wolfgang Köhler calls his "neglect to change, to appease, to redeem the world."[6] Given Hofmannsthal's view of the connection between world and individual, the fate of the merchant's son is probably most accurately described as the result of betrayal of the self. Assuming that Uwe Böker is right when he says that the *Tale of the Merchant's Son and His Servants* treats the basic Hofmannsthal theme of search for identity,[7] then that betrayal consists specifically in finding identity and refusing to accept it.

Hofmannsthal's more famous *Reitergeschichte* (*Horseman Story*; published in 1908) is framed in historically identifiable circumstances. The time is 1848. The situation is the war waged by the Austrians against the Italian Liberation Army.

On the surface, the story describes the events leading up to the execution of Sergeant Major Anton Lerch for insubordination. It is the deeper causes of that insubordination, however, that are of primary interest to us here.

Lerch makes the mistake of following inclinations that lead him away from his duty to himself. First, memories distract him from the responsibilities of his orderly military life. While riding through Milan after a series of successful skirmishes, Lerch recognizes a woman whom he had known some years before. He is immediately drawn to her. Rather than disciplining the longing for civilian life that wells up within him, he slips away from the squadron, apparently unnoticed. In so doing, he symbolically forsakes the identity of an honorable non-commissioned officer. Richard Alewyn points up the significance of Lerch's action in the following words: "In that one unguarded moment, in which he lets his glance stray away, and, giving in to a private curiosity, leaves his unit to enter a house situated near the street, he is done for."[8]

Although Lerch returns almost immediately, a perceptible change has begun to take place within him. He is no longer a committed soldier, but has mentally projected himself into "an atmosphere of comfort and pleasant violence without a service assignment." His heretofore dormant baser self has begun to stir.

The critical phase of Lerch's transformation comes next as a direct consequence of the encounter with the woman Vuic. The stimulus of what he has seen and the monotony of the ensuing ride promote a mental transition from remembrance to dream. His daydreams in turn make him vulnerable to aroused internal drives. Specifically, he is seized with "a thirst for unexpected profit, for gratifications, for ducats falling suddenly into his pocket."

The wish to earn "a totally extraordinary bonus" carries Lerch, again without authorization, away from his squadron. This time a nearby village lures him. It is a squalid, repelling place, the diametrical opposite of the beautiful Milan where he first went astray—a reflection, incidentally, of Hofmannsthal's own impressions of backward towns encountered during his military service. In a sense, the ride through the wayside town is an excursion into Lerch's now degenerate self. In Volker Durr's words, the village is "the projection of his chaotic insides."[9] It represents his total submersion in the mire of self-indulgence.

For Lerch, the dilapidated village is a nightmare. Everything seems oriented toward forcing him to remain in that environment. Animals and people block his way.

His horse seems to move in slow motion. The smallest details are forcibly imposed upon his senses. Finally, however, Lerch reaches a bridge at the end of the village. There an extremely important confrontation takes place as his double rides toward him from the other side.

The face-to-face meeting between Lerch and his double is for critics the most controversial part of the story. Ulrich Heimrath, for example, sees Lerch's attempt to ward off the spectre as the refusal to let knowledge of the self become a working force within him.[10] Alewyn maintains that the double fills its traditional folklore role as a messenger of death.[11] William R. Donlop goes so far as to interpret it as dead Lerch's ghost "who returns from the not too distant future."[12]

All of these interpretations have in common the perception of the double as a manifestation of Lerch's self with which he is not able to cope. In that respect, they are all correct. But there are other details of the incident to be taken into account.

Lerch's double comes from the other side of the bridge, from where his squadron is about to engage the enemy once more. The double can thus be viewed more as a messenger from the past than the future. One can take the position that the double represents the sergeant major's old, honorable military identity, the identity that Lerch must take up again if he is to survive under the conditions that will obtain once he rejoins his unit. By rejecting the other self, as he symbolically does by raising his arm against the apparition, Lerch confirms the new dominance of his baser nature.

In the skirmish that follows, Lerch succeeds in getting his "unexpected profit," a beautiful horse whose rider he has slain. When Baron Rofrano, Lerch's commanding officer, orders that the captured horse be released along with others taken during the fight, Lerch rebels. His reaction is described thus: "And from a depth of his soul unknown even to himself, a bestial anger mounted against the man there before him who intended to take the horse from him, a terrible anger toward the face, the voice, the bearing, and the whole existence of this man, such as can only arise in a mysterious fashion through years of living close together."

The old Lerch would have obeyed Rofrano immediately. The new Lerch is a slave to his lower instincts. He therefore refuses, and Rofrano nonchalantly puts a bullet through his head. Lerch's new-found identity dooms him. By allowing it to dominate him, Lerch actually commits suicide.

An unfinished novel, *Andreas, oder die Vereinigten* (Andreas, or the United), portrays the coming to grips with one's self as a constructive process. Perhaps that is what troubled Hofmannsthal about the "problematic fragments" of "this possibly all too daring work" and made it so difficult for him to complete.[13]

Andreas is openly patterned after Goethe's *Wilhelm Meister*. In the fragment Hofmannsthal equates the search for identity with the general process of maturation.

The framework of the novel is an educational journey. The year is 1778. Young Andreas von Ferschengelder travels from Vienna to Venice to further his personal development. In Villach, an obnoxious person named Gotthilff persuades the inexperienced Andreas to hire him as a servant. While they are riding, Gotthilff's horse goes lame. Thus they are compelled to stop at a farm owned by the Finazzer family. There Andreas falls in love with Romana, the daughter of his host.

Unfortunately, the budding love affair is frustrated by Gotthilff's treachery. One night Gotthilff, after assaulting one of the Finazzers' maids, absconds with Andreas's horse and half of his money. Disgraced by the actions of his servant, Andreas leaves the farm by wagon two days later.

Upon his arrival in Venice, Andreas finds lodgings
in the house of Count Prampero, a poverty-stricken nobleman. The kindly Prampero earns a living by snuffing
out the lamps in the theater across the street; his wife is
an usher.

Andreas soon becomes involved with the younger
daughter of the Pramperos, Zustina. She is in the process
of sponsoring a lottery to raise funds for her family. First
prize is to be her virginity. Andreas is politely informed
that because he is a stranger he will not be allowed to
purchase a ticket. But Zorzi, an artist who lives in the
house, offers to try and get one for him anonymously.

Zorzi also volunteers to introduce Andreas to Nina,
the older Prampero daughter, who lives by herself as a
coquette. On the way to her apartment, the two men stop
at a coffeehouse, where Andreas meets the mysterious
Maltese Knight Sacramozo. Then, while he is waiting
outside Nina's for Zorzi to announce his visit, Andreas
has two strange encounters.

In front of a small church Andreas sees a young
woman who stares at him. When he follows her into the
church, she turns and seems to approach him, her arms
raised in a silent plea, then sinks down upon a prie-dieu.
Andreas decides to leave, but turns once more to look at
her. To his amazement a different woman now stands by
the prie-dieu and beckons to him. When he disregards her
gestures and walks out of the church, an attractive young
girl brushes past him from behind and disappears over a
small bridge.

As Zorzi has still not returned, Andreas wanders
into a nearby courtyard. Atop a wall he sees the face of
still another woman peering at him seductively. A hand
reaches out toward him, but then face and hand disappear. He then searches in vain for the unknown woman.

After the encounter with Nina, which proves to be a
disappointment, Andreas returns to the church, hoping to

find some trace of the mysterious woman. The church, however, is now quite empty. At this point the fragment ends.

Initially, Andreas views his journey to Venice as simply the fulfillment of his parents' desire that he "get acquainted with foreign people, observe foreign customs, and perfect his own behavior." Later he becomes aware that a deeper, more abiding necessity has made the trip imperative. In Venice he recalls an instance during the journey when "even he was not quite sure who he was." Consequently, all subsequent events become a part of the quest for understanding of that elusive self.

Actually Hofmannsthal intended Andreas ultimately to use his experiences in order to expand his awareness of self beyond the normal limits. As Fritz Martini sees it, the goal of Andreas's educational journey is "not so much the development of an individual on the basis of his psychological characteristics. Nor is it the dovetailing of the individual into a rigidly outlined social destiny, nor the development of a self to the peak of its powers or to pass a practical active test within human society. Rather, it goes beyond all of this. It is a matter of the formation of an ego that feels within itself its security only as inhibitions, its powers only as unconscious and still unformed, still intangible possibilities."[14]

In the completed sections of the novel, Andreas gradually discovers some fragments of his identity. Martini says this about it: "Andreas is a man divided, not only between dreams and reality, between self and world, but also, even within himself, between possibilities that appear to cancel one another and, in the search for realization and decision, to hinder each other in their fulfillment."[15] Hofmannsthal's notes suggest, however, that Andreas would eventually overcome this lack of integration and arrive at a lasting internal and external harmony.

As might be expected, Andreas's various identities

correspond to the major metaphors that Hofmannsthal
used for life: man as a dreamer, as a player of games,
and as an actor. Andreas gains insight into self and his
relationship to others by variously assuming these identities through individual free decisions. He thereby has experiences that expand both the world within him and his
outward sphere of influence.

At least one facet of Andreas's total identity sur-
faces before he even arrives in Venice. It occurs during
his experiences with Gotthilff. It is Gotthilff who awakens
the dreamer in Andreas and the first glimmerings of
awareness of what his journey is really all about. Gotthilff
does this by identifying and taking advantage of aspects
of Andreas's being of which the latter is not even aware.
Richard Alewyn gives an appropriate assessment of
Gotthilff's hold on Andreas when he says: "When he
[Andreas] was unable to shake off his satanic com-
panion, when against his will he had to allow Gotthilff so
much power over himself, this happened because the
other understood with infamous sureness how to detect
Andreas's most secret weaknesses and vulnerabilities and
how to ally himself with the dreams and drives that
slumbered unknown and untamed deep within him."[16]

Thus, when Gotthilff brags about his amorous ex-
ploits, Andreas dreams of playing the lover. "He thought
of how it would be if he was to arrive this evening at
Pormberg Castle, and he was expected and other guests
as well. It is the evening after a hunt, and he is the best
shot. Wherever he aims, something falls. The beautiful
countess who is in his vicinity, when he shoots, plays with
him with her glance like he toys with the lives of the
forest animals."

Similarly, when Gotthilff eventually steals Andreas's
horse, his saddle, and half his money, revealing himself
as a criminal, Andreas internalizes that facet of Gotthilff
and at one point sees himself as "a criminal and murderer
like Gotthilff." It is at least partially because he senses

something of Gotthilff within himself, that he feels such
extreme guilt at Gotthilff's outrages. "To Andreas it
seemed as though he had done something serious, and
now everything was coming to light."

On the whole, however, Gotthilff's contribution to
Andreas's development is positive. He brings Andreas to
the Finazzer estate, where for the first time Andreas becomes aware that he must absorb external relationships
into his own being. Only within him can they become a
part of unquestioned reality.

The major example of Andreas's development in
this regard is his love for Romana. The permanence of
their union, despite what has happened, is revealed to
Andreas in a dream that enables him to reconcile himself
to the impending separation made necessary by Gotthilff's
treachery. Concerning his reaction to the dream we
read: "He knew that he had dreamed, but the truth in the
dream let happiness pulse through all the veins in his
body. Romana's entire being had revealed itself to him
with a life that was beyond reality. Everything difficult
was blown away. Within him or outside him he could not
lose her. . . . His body was a temple in which Romana's
essence dwelt."

At the Finazzer estate all of Andreas's experiences
become unique extensions of himself, and the things that
take place inside him have the special quality of simul-
taneity. For that reason, his dreams are a peculiar mixture of past and present. In one instance, for example, he
dreams of Romana along with a dog whose back he had
broken with an angry kick during childhood.

At the same time, the future is also alive within him.
He lies in his room at night, aware of Romana's parents
nearby, and thinks to himself: "That is my house one
day, my wife. Thus will I lie next to her and talk about
our children."

This transition to partial self-awareness is by no

means easy for Andreas. At first he rejects what he learns. His perception degenerates to a confusion of fragments similar to that described by Lord Chandos in his letter to Francis Bacon.[17] Thus, one evening at dinner Andreas's sense impressions are "like never before in his life, everything as though it was chopped up: darkness and light, the faces and the hands." Later, under increasing pressure, he tries to flee into the fragmented universe. "At last he had escaped from himself, as from a prison. He rushed away in leaps. He knew nothing of himself but the moment." At the grave of a dog that Gotthilff had poisoned, however, Andreas recognizes the futility of his attempted flight from reality. " 'Here,' he said aloud, 'here! All that running around is useless. You cannot run away from yourself.' "

In Venice, Andreas assumes other identities. One of the most obvious is that of a game player. He becomes a player of games in response to stimuli from his immediate surroundings. The first person he meets in Venice is "a hopeless gambler," who, in finding Andreas a room with the Pramperos, indirectly introduces him to the rather peculiar situation brought about by Zustina's virginity lottery. Hofmannsthal's notes on the unfinished portion of the novel reveal that Zustina would rig the lottery in favor of Andreas, who had acquired a ticket, in an effort to establish a lasting relationship with him. Incidentally, the lottery is symbolic for Zustina's view of men. In her eyes, men are all either "family tyrants or players of all kinds."

Another consequence of Andreas's rooming with the Pramperos is the realization of one of his fondest desires. In Vienna he had always wanted to live near a theater. Now the Saint Samuel Theater is right across the street, and moreover, the entire household works there. No immediate opportunity arises for Andreas to become active in the world of the stage because he himself is not

ready. He is so unsure of the propriety of such a course
that he even decides not to inform his parents that the
theater is nearby.

Nevertheless, Andreas participates in a broad sense
as a front-row spectator in Hofmannsthal's metaphor of
life as theater. He therefore experiences life in Venice as
"an intellectual masquerade, full of erotic depths and
superficialities."[18] The most obvious examples of this
are his encounters with the mysterious women in the
church and courtyard while waiting for Zorzi to introduce
him to Nina.

Although the full significance of the episode in the
church is not apparent, some information about it can be
gleaned from Hofmannsthal's notes. Apparently, the person Andreas encounters is a young schizophrenic Spanish
woman whose dual personalities are named Maria and
Mariquita. Given that information, the encounter becomes an experience involving the psychological extreme
in role-playing, the individual who is literally more than
one person.

What Hofmannsthal intended to do with Maria-
Mariquita cannot be fully determined. One can only say
that, because of the experience in the church, she becomes a part of Andreas's world and hence of Andreas
himself. Moreover, Andreas senses that she is important,
even though he may not yet be aware that the problem of
man's multiple nature is inseparably connected with his
own future. In the novel Hofmannsthal describes Andreas's continuing awareness of her in these words: "The
thought of this unknown woman assailed him, but like a
dread. This being was in the world. Therein lay something that was inescapable."

Although Hofmannsthal did not detail the unfolding
of Andreas's own actor nature in the fragment, there are
suggestions in his notes that Andreas was to mature as an
actor by modeling himself after the Maltese Knight Sacramozo. In one place Hofmannsthal wrote: "In the com-

pany of the Maltese Knight, indeed only through a relationship to him, Andreas's existence purifies and collects itself."[19] What is most important is that Andreas is eventually to recognize in Sacramozo "a master of the playing of his own role."[20] Hofmannsthal obviously intended for Andreas to gain that same mastery.

In the final analysis then, it would be Sacramozo's influence that would give Andreas the final push into what Manfred Hoppe has called "inexpressible union" with the world.[21] In one of the notes Hofmannsthal has Sacramozo tell Andreas: "Everything perfects itself in circles. Much escapes us, and yet it is in us, and we need only understand how to work it forth."[22] It is this "knowledge of the secret of human organization,"[23] that Hofmannsthal intended Sacramozo to contribute to Andreas's development. With Sacramozo's help, Andreas could then take this last step: "His senses become refined, he feels himself more capable of enjoying the individual in the other man, feels himself to be more an individual and a higher one."[24] In short, through contact with Sacramozo, Andreas could ultimately embrace the whole of his own identity.

4

Life Is a Drama

To Hofmannsthal the stage was more than an artistic construct symbolic of life. Theater was life itself as he felt and experienced it. In a letter to Leopold von Andrian of May 4, 1896, Hofmannsthal revealed how much the idea of acting out a role had already merged with his personal psychological existence. He wrote: "I return to myself like one who has been incessantly play-acting, acting out a role to be sure that is mysteriously patterned after one's own nature but a role nonetheless. That is probably nonsense but of the sort from which I cannot escape. These imaginings form the background for my world."[1] As a result of this attitude, all of Hofmannsthal's creations for the stage, from the firstling *Yesterday* to *The Tower*, became "life-dramas."[2]

The most important early example of Hofmannsthal's theatrical development of the life-is-a-drama theme is *Der Tor und der Tod* (Death and the Fool,) which was written in 1894. This work became Hofmannsthal's best-known and best-loved short lyric play.

The tragedy of Claudio, the fool, is that of the individual who has failed properly to appreciate and play his role. He is therefore not prepared when the time comes for him to die. Claudio's problem is that he has preferred to be a spectator rather than an actor in the theater of life. For that reason, he has never really tasted what life has to offer. Shortly before Death appears to summon him from the stage, Claudio says:

What do I know about human life?
Of course, I've seemed to stand within it,
But then at most I've studied it,
Could never mingle myself in it.

Because of this gnawing awareness that he has remained an outsider, Claudio tries to reject Death's sum-
mons. "But I have not lived!" he argues. Death, however,
remains unsympathetic. His only concession is to grant
Claudio a brief respite in order to teach him "to honor
life for once" before he leaves it.

One by one three figures return from the dead to
accuse Claudio: his mother, a young girl whom he had
mistreated, and a friend who had loved the girl. The
reproaches of the three are summed up by the friend, who
says he is happier in death than the living Claudio because Claudio means nothing to anyone, and nobody
means anything to him. Finally, Claudio must acknowledge that his life has been a miserable failure:

As on the stage a bad comedian passes,
He comes on cue, recites his part and goes
Indifferent to all that's not himself
Not even moved by hearing his own voice,
Nor do his hollow tones move any others:
So too across this greater stage of life
I've moved without conviction, strength, or worth.

Although he then seems to reconcile himself to dying,
there is no mistaking the haunting lament of his final
speech with its tragic line: "Only dying, do I feel that I
exist."

Most of Hofmannsthal's life-dramas compare and
contrast different types of people. *Das kleine Welttheater*
(The Little Theater of the World,) written in 1897, does
this by presenting a poet, a gardener, a girl, and a mad-
man, among others, who perform what can best be described as a kind of round dance. Each figure stops once
on a bridge in the center of the stage and delivers a

monologue that characterizes his or her situation in life.

The most important character in *The Little Theater of the World* is the fool. Ironically, it is he who has the deepest insights into life. And only he fully recognizes life for the drama that it is. The fool's servant puts it in these words, as he describes his master:

> Gentle, for the sake of a mere drama
> He believes, he stays inside his body,
> Which he can discard whene'er he pleases
> Drop as from the rim of some small vessel
> Down into the stream, and if he wanted,
> Pass into the trunk of yonder maple,
> Climb into the stalks of reeds and rushes.

These lines present in symbols Hofmannsthal's personal view that in the absolute realm man is a player of many and diverse roles. By attributing these ideas to a fool, Hofmannsthal took a quick jab at the way his opinions on the nature of existence were received by his contemporaries.

Regardless of the diversity of character types, the players of all roles in the drama of life must, like Claudio, experience the confrontation with death. Hofmannsthal viewed death itself as a positive occurrence. From his perspective, any negative aspects of the experience were purely subjective, purely an "inherited dread" like that which Death attributes to Claudio.

Jedermann (Everyman), which Hofmannsthal wrote in 1911, was a major attempt to capture the essence of the death experience and to remind the world of what he believed would ensure a happy death. Basically, the message of Hofmannsthal's *Everyman* is that this life is part of something greater, that the world is only one transient stage, and that, for our actions in it, we shall all be called to account on the day of judgment. The story is derived from a medieval English morality play, also titled *Everyman*.

Everyman is summoned before God to give an accounting for his life. His dealings with others before Death's arrival on the scene are contrasted with his attempts to get someone to go with him, once he knows that his time has come. His friends and his money, of course, leave him no choice but to rely on Faith and Good Works. These eventually enable him, despite weakness and initial unwillingness, to repent and put his life in order, thus saving him from the devil.

Hofmannsthal's view of what he had accomplished with *Everyman* differed sharply from that of many critics. The young Bertolt Brecht accused him of "indescribably amateurish tastelessness."[3] Others felt that Hofmannsthal, by using the story from the old English morality play, used an art form that could not really be revived successfully. Hofmannsthal thought that his attackers were underestimating him because they had neglected to compare his play with the English classic. In a letter to Richard Strauss of December 1913, Hofmannsthal insisted: "It [a comparison] would have shown them that I have not simply added a few fingers to an old wooden sculpture, but that I have added—not without poetic vocation, I think—a whole body to its one hand and what was at best half a mutilated head."[4]

In some respects at least, Hofmannsthal's critics were justified in their negative reaction to the play. *Everyman* has one obvious weakness: its artificiality. The piousness of the play is more sentimental than sincere. Everyman's redemption at the end comes across as forced because it lacks sufficient justification. Even the rhymed doggerel verse, with all its simplicity, conveys the impression of conscious construction. Nevertheless, with respect to the ultimate success of the play, these weaknesses proved to be unimportant. The author perceived correctly that there was great strength in the undying Christian allegory itself. By clothing that allegory in appropriate color and pageantry, Hofmannsthal succeeded in creating a drama that has continued to captivate audiences since the first performance in front of the Salzburg cathedral.

An objective comparison of Hofmannsthal's version with the English Everyman, however, reveals that while he did add new elements, his changes were not as drastic as he would have us believe. The two major innovations are a colorful banqueting scene that Max Reinhardt suggested, and a scene at the end in which the devil is cheated out of Everyman's soul. (The latter segment appears to be patterned after a similar situation in the second part of Goethe's *Faust*.)

Everyman was a significant preliminary study for Hofmannsthal's most important life-drama, *Das Salzburger grosse Welttheater* (The Salzburg Great Theater of the World). Written in 1922, it benefited directly from the treatment of several problems in *Everyman*. These include: the question of free agency, the need for positive action, man's role in society, and the appropriate attitude toward death. Hofmannsthal's previous elucidation of these questions enabled him to expand and perfect his treatment of them in the later play. And that despite the fact that *The Salzburg Great Theater of the World* is also an adaptation of older material.

The stage metaphor employed in *The Salzburg Great Theater of the World* is taken expressly from Calderón's *El gran teatro del mundo*. In his preface to *The Salzburg Great Theater of the World*, Hofmannsthal describes the connection between the two dramas as follows: "All the world knows that there is a religious play by Calderón entitled *The Great Theater of the World*. From it is borrowed here the metaphor that supports the whole: that the world builds a stage upon which people present the play of life in the roles given them by God; in addition, the title of that play and the names of the six figures by whom humanity is represented—otherwise nothing." Although the assertion contained in the last two words is something of an exaggeration, it is quite clear that the two plays have distinct differences.

For one thing, in Hofmannsthal's play, the portion of the action that takes place in the premortal realm receives a much greater emphasis than it does in Calderón's play. The general scheme of Calderón's drama was especially attractive to Hofmannsthal because it readily lent itself to a detailed elaboration on the idea of "preexistence."[5] When Hofmannsthal had attempted to develop the preexistence concept in his opera *Die Frau ohne Schatten* (The Woman without a Shadow), the public had not understood what he was trying to say. This is a tale about a fairy empress who becomes human by achieving motherhood and accepting her role as "the bridge, stretched across the abyss,/upon which the dead once more cross into life." It has its charms. But theatergoers had difficulty in relating it to their own lives. *The Salzburg Great Theater of the World* allowed Hofmannsthal to present his ideas on preexistence in a clearer form, thus enabling the reader or spectator to identify more easily with what was being offered.

Accordingly, a major difference between Hofmannsthal's work and that of Calderón lies in the treatment of the unborn actor-souls. Calderón portrays them as more or less passive and uniform, without distinctive characteristics except as contained in the assigned roles. Hofmannsthal, on the other hand, endows the unborn souls themselves with individuality. More important, Hofmannsthal's figures are capable of making free-will decisions. Indeed they insist upon that right.

The concept of free agency is crucial to Hofmannsthal's play. As the Master instructs the World as to what he expects, he says that the drama of life must be "a living, secret, free operation." For that reason, an angel emphasizes to the actor-souls the importance of how they play the role as opposed to the nature of the role itself:

"Not a role, but the play itself will be called good or bad
when things have reached their end; and this not because of
his role—may he have had the beggar's staff in his hands or
the king's sword and scepter—rather because of what he
made of the role, will one or more be called to the Master's
table—but a bungler will be viewed unfavorably by his
Master, and there is no correcting later, where one failed on
the stage."

From the outset then, the unborn souls are subject
to two major conditions. They are given "a spark of the
highest freedom," and they are made responsible for how
they exercise it.

In the opening scene, in the realm of preexistence,
Hofmannsthal offers his answer to the idea of predestina-
tion. The Adversary argues that by assigning the souls
specific roles, the Master robs the souls of their freedom
and in essence plays "with puppets that hang from wires
in his hands." In spite of the Master's denial, one soul
initially views its role from the same perspective. The
actor-soul who is to play the Beggar rejects that role at
first, saying: "Give me a role in which there is freedom,
as much as one needs in order not to suffocate, or leave
me out of the play." An angel tries to persuade the rebel-
lious spirit to accept the role as an opportunity to act,
insisting: "Action alone is creation above creation."

The unconvinced soul responds: "You say, action?
My soul thirsts for action! Where in this miserable role
would there be room for a single action?" Only when the
soul becomes convinced that it will have the chance to
act on its own, does it make the decision to accept the
role.

As one might suspect from this beginning, the Beggar's role is of major importance to Hofmannsthal's exposition of Calderón's life-drama material. Hanns Hammelmann puts the role of the Beggar into its proper perspective when he says that Hofmannsthal was justified in
claiming the play as his own, despite its having been

derived from Calderón's play "because the powerful *active* figure of the beggar here gives the play an entirely new dramatic meaning and climax."[6] In Calderón's play, the Beggar is exalted at the end because of the things that he has suffered. Not so with Hofmannsthal's version. His Beggar is rewarded for the way he plays a difficult role, for his positive exercise of free agency.

The action of the segment of the play that depicts mortality is quite straightforward up to the point at which the Beggar performs his decisive act. The King takes Beauty and Wisdom to his side, honors the Rich Man, and provides in his realm an appropriate place for the Peasant. The figures follow their own inclinations and neglect the real purpose of the play, as it was outlined to them in the premortal state. This draws a sharp reminder from an angel:

> Give heed unto the play
> In which you stand, and how its title sounded once.
> The Lord is over you! Do not forget its course.

Finally, the Beggar appears. Unlike the Rich Man, who consistently responds to the promptings of the Adversary, the Beggar takes full responsibility for his words and actions. When the Adversary tries to coach him, he says: "Be still! I've found my words within myself./I need no advocate."

Apparently accepting employment as a woodsman in the Peasant's forest, the Beggar picks up an ax. Suddenly he turns on the others and threatens to destroy them and take power for himself, arguing in a very modern way that all their privileges are stolen.

To this point the actions of the players have been dictated by their own lower natures. They have failed to regard the words of angels prompting them from the wings. Just as the Beggar raises his ax, however, he sees a vision that causes him to exercise his will against his initial inclination. By staying his hand, he performs the

positive action for which he had longed in the realm of
preexistence. This fact is confirmed by an angel.

> You craved for deeds, soul, in your role!
> Deluded, you were near misdeed.
> Yet now the play is glorious!
> Not misdeed, deed has now been done!

For the Beggar, the major consequence of his deed
is that while still in the mortal sphere he regains consciousness of his true identity as an actor on the stage of
life. Thus, when the Adversary tries to goad him again
toward destructive violence, he is able to respond:

> I am with God amid all of these things,
> But in the play I am the Beggar now
> Whose form and nature I have taken on.
> What should I therefore want of them?
> I surely cannot now assume their roles
> Nor yet include their lines and leaps in mine!

This outlook then makes it possible for him to face death
happily, knowing that once he leaves the stage he will
appear before the Master as he really is.

The Beggar's act of conversion is more than a
simple assertion of free will. It symbolizes an internal
transformation that Hofmannsthal thought was necessary
for the people of his own time, a transformation that
could only result from positive action. After the horrors
of World War I, Hofmannsthal was extremely disturbed
by the attitudes of selfishness and cynicism that he encountered. He regarded *The Salzburg Great Theater of
the World* as a healing experience to the ills of society.
As he expressed it in a letter to a close friend: "I cannot
complain about the death of a human being. It rather
saddens me that people make such wretched use of their
lives. When I read to you the ending of the *World Theater*, you will understand what I mean."[7]

From a dramatic point of view, there is one significant weakness in the play and that perhaps not without

reason. For all Hofmannsthal's good intentions, the sudden change in the Beggar comes off as artificial. Richard Strauss pinpointed the trouble, when he wrote in a letter of 1922: "However beautiful the idea of the sudden conversion of the Beggar may be poetically, to my dramatic feeling there is still a jarring crack intervening between the true dramatic solution (i.e., the completion of the destruction) and the Christian concept of sudden change of heart. . . . Your Beggar does not act true to character right up to the end, but is at the critical moment illumined by Hofmannsthal."[8]

In spite of such negative critical appraisal, however, *The Salzburg Great Theater of the World* became on the stage one of Hofmannsthal's most popular plays.

A major component of all Hofmannsthal's life-dramas is social criticism. *Everyman* questions the desirability of a society in which Mammon can turn the individual into his "well-behaved jumping jack." The arguments of the Beggar in *The Salzburg Great Theater of the World* cast doubt upon the validity of the modern social order as a whole. It is therefore not surprising that the life-dramas are closely related to other Hofmannsthal plays of a more pronounced social bent, especially the comedies.

In his essay on *Der Schwierige* (The Difficult Man), Emil Staiger has observed that comedy is the form of life "that is played in every get-together, unavoidably, even though it only seldom enters consciousness."[9] In other words, comedy is man playing the role of himself in the social context. It is precisely in this light that Hofmannsthal saw his own comedies.

The most important aspect of Hofmannsthal's development of the man-is-an-actor notion is that an individual plays his best and happiest role when playing himself. In that sense, the playing of a role modeled after one's own nature is a variation on the problem of the search for identity. That is, a person succeeds in estab-

lishing his identity in direct proportion to the facility with
which he plays the appropriate role.

A good illustration is the figure of Zdenka in *Arabella*. As the younger daughter of parents who cannot
afford to finance the social amenities for two girls at
once, she is forced by her mother to play the male role of
Zdenko. She plays the role well for a time, but eventually
provides herself with an opportunity to be the girl that
she is. Her sister Arabella refuses to respond favorably to
Matteo, an officer who is in love with her. Zdenka therefore poses as Arabella in a darkened room and gives
Matteo the affection she thinks he deserves. When the
masquerade is exposed, Zdenka finds happiness with
Matteo as a result of having revealed her true nature
while playing Arabella.

Hofmannsthal even made the ability to play oneself a
consideration in his evaluation of professional actors.
The best tribute he could pay to the great actress Sarah
Bernhardt was: "She plays herself: the refined mood
poetry of her limbs, the tragicomedy of her nerves, the
animal rush of her passions."[10]

Similarly, where the role of actor appears as a part
in one of his own works, Hofmannsthal presents as best
that actor who plays himself. One example is the actress
Zerbinetta in the opera *Ariadne on Naxos*. A special person is needed to meet the demands of a very peculiar
kind of stage situation. A wealthy patron has insisted that
a burlesque comedy be played simultaneously on the
same stage with the tragedy of Ariadne, the daughter of
King Minos of Crete who, abandoned on a desert island
by Theseus, longs for death. The comedy and tragedy are
to be combined and performed without rehearsal. Zerbinetta is a match for these conditions because, as one of
the other characters puts it, "she is a master at improvis-
ing; since she always plays only herself, she finds her way
in every situation."

In Hofmannsthal's treatments of the life-is-a-drama

theme, problems arise when an individual refuses to play himself or when those around him decline to accept his role. In either case, the inevitable result is misunderstanding. In *The Difficult Man* such misunderstandings form the basis for what the renowned critic Wilhelm Emrich has called "the most perfect comedy of the twentieth century."[11]

The scene is Vienna after World War I. Hans Karl Bühl, the central character, has successfully avoided marriage and thereby thwarted his sister Crescence's plans for him. His nephew Stani imitates him because he sees in Hans Karl the ability to play "the great gentleman" effortlessly, though Hans Karl himself is an unassuming man who dislikes the social limelight.

Despite the fact that he has succeeded his uncle as Antoinette Hechingen's lover, Stani intends to marry Helene Altenwyl. At Crescence's request, Hans Karl agrees to attend a party at Altenwyls and put in a good word for Stani with Helene. At the same time Hans Karl hopes to mediate a reconciliation between Antoinette Hechingen and her husband. Rather than help either cause, he only creates confusion. Instead of proposing for Stani he inadvertently reveals his own love for Helene, then flees. When he returns to ask Helene to forget what he said, she proposes to him.

The misunderstandings in the play arise because of Hans Karl's handling of his own role and his reactions to the conscious roles played by others. Initially, "the difficult man" refuses to let his true self show through the mask. So long as he hides behind the mask, others get an inaccurate view of him. Once he is drawn into the social context, however, circumstances force his inner nature into the open with tragicomic repercussions.

Ironically, the authentic Hans Karl emerges only after Hans Karl has been confronted with a caricature of himself. Just before the Altenwyl party, Hans Karl goes to the circus and watches the clown Furlani. When he comes to the party, he can think of nothing else. He thus begins to act the part of the clown. Furlani, as Hans Karl thinks of him, "plays his role; he is the one whom everyone understands, who wants to help everyone and in so doing brings everything into the greatest confusion." In Hans Karl's case, however, much of the ensuing confusion results from the fact that others do not understand him in the Furlani role.

The scene involving Antoinette Hechingen is a good example. Hans Karl was once her lover. She interprets his coming to the party as a positive response to an overture for reconciliation that she had made through her maid. When hard-to-get Hans Karl turns into an advocate of the order, security, and propriety of marriage, and encourages her to return to her husband, Antoinette is not only disappointed. She simply cannot comprehend what is going on.

By the same token, when he plays himself, Hans Karl fails to have regard for the roles others have put on for *his* benefit. As a result, he sees through them without intending to do so. That is, he involuntarily exposes the people who seek to unmask him, to interpret him, to place him within the social context. Once unmasked, the other characters are also forced to play their real selves, and each then contributes in his own way to the growing turmoil.

Of all Hofmannsthal's dramatic figures, Hans Karl Bühl is unquestionably among the most human and therefore the most complicated. More than anything else he successfully illustrates that "the difficult man" is an appropriate appellation for man, the actor. After all, as Hofmannsthal allows the World to observe at one point in *The Salzburg Great Theater of the World*, actors "are difficult people."

5

Life Is a Game

Yesterday, the first of Hofmannsthal's short lyric dramas, introduced the young writer's audience to a character type that was to continue to intrigue him until his death. Although shallow and passive, Andrea is one progenitor of a diverse series of players of the game of life. He lives "between game and feast," and devotes his time to bragging, playing, drinking, and laughing, to "what one does with men, when one is not fighting." Structured on a slight theme—of Andrea's discovery that Arlette, his girlfriend, was unfaithful to him the day before—*Yesterday* gives us little more than a brief glimpse of the gameplayers to come. In effect, Andrea is a weak grandfather to characters whose father is another, more powerful figure, the archetype of the life-game player, Casanova.

Hofmannsthal closely patterned the leading roles for two major dramas after material from Casanova's memoirs. One of the roles was that of Baron Weidenstamm, the mature man of the world of *Der Abenteurer und die Sängerin* (The Adventurer and the Singer; 1917). The other was Florindo, the young libertine of *Cristina's Trip Home*. (Florindo is also the protagonist of a fragmentary early version of that play, which was published independently in 1923 under the title *Florindo*.) In a letter of August 1908 to Count Harry Kessler, Hofmannsthal defined their relationships to Casanova when he asked:

"Isn't Florindo just as nice a cover name for the young Casanova as Weidenstamm was for the old one?"[1]

Several other Hofmannsthal figures also bear an unmistakable family resemblance to Casanova. Among the most obvious offspring are the Baron, from the fragmentary comedy *Sylvia in the Star*, and Jaromir, the playful young husband in *The Incorruptible Man*.

Like *Yesterday*, *The Adventurer and the Singer* is a work written at the time when Hofmannsthal was still struggling with the fine points of dramatic technique. Consequently, the play lacks much of the polish and flair of later works. That fact caused the socialist critic Franz Mehring to make a rather harsh assessment of the young author's potential. Based on his evaluation of *The Adventurer and the Singer* and *Die Hochzeit der Sobeide*, 1899 (The Marriage of Sobeide), another of Hofmannsthal's early dramas, Mehring wrote: "This talent is completely lacking in greatness and strength, in original impulse and fury; one might call it an impeccably clothed fop, but a fop nevertheless."[2] Although Hofmannsthal later proved Mehring to be wrong, it is nevertheless clear that for all his demonstrated literary ability, the young Hofmannsthal was not the born master of the drama that he was of the lyric poem.

Still, *The Adventurer and the Singer* is important for at least two reasons. It gives us a good picture of the Hofmannsthal adventurer as a basic human type, and it is the author's first major expansion of the game metaphor *per se*.

The play is constructed around an encounter between the middle-aged Casanova figure Weidenstamm and a mistress, Vittoria, whom he has not seen for many years. In the meantime, Vittoria has married Lorenzo Venier. Unexpectedly, Vittoria revives their earlier relationship in all its depth by introducing Weidenstamm to a son whom he had never known. Until now she has successfully passed off the young Cesarino as her brother.

When Venier becomes suspicious because of the sharp resemblance between Cesarino and a picture of Weidenstamm in his youth, Vittoria continues the deception by admitting that Weidenstamm is Cesarino's father but insisting that she and Cesarino are nevertheless brother and sister. She simply claims that she and the boy had two different fathers. Pacified, Venier accepts the explanation. Further complication of the matter is averted when Weidenstamm is forced to leave the city. Another of his earlier paramours has recognized him and threatens to expose him to the authorities.

The game metaphor is entrenched as much in the background as in the action of the play. Even time and place contribute to the overall game atmosphere. With reference to *The Adventurer and the Singer*, Günther Erken has pointed out that the game of chance "gives Venice of the eighteenth century its coloring. Gaming is an ingredient, almost the essence of this world."[3] Accordingly, the drama begins in Casanova's domain at an evening gambling party. During the first half of the play, the supporting characters circulate on the stage between two focal points: Weidenstamm, the embodiment of game playing, and the gaming table itself.

Weidenstamm characterizes himself—and thereby both Hofmannsthal's game-player as a type and the nature of the game—in two significant speeches. In the first he defines the stakes for which he plays, that is, the grand prize of the game of life. He says: "We commit the greatest inanities for the sake of a woman whom we have seen in passing; and in order to open the laces of a bodice, we stake our lives without hesitating a moment, even before we know what the bodice hides." In other words, the player of this particular game characteristically wagers himself against a greater portion of life, whatever that portion may be. That the self is indeed an implement of the game, a sort of toy, is reinforced once more symbolically when Weidenstamm makes Venier a present of a box with a painted miniature of himself upon the lid, and calls it "a plaything."

The second significant speech reveals how Weiden-stamm himself has played the game. As he meets with Vittoria for the last time and realizes that he will not see Cesarino again, Weidenstamm hands her a ring and says:

> "Give him the ring, and with it tell him this:
> It comes from one, who with a thousand arms
> Reached out for all life's pleasures; like a child
> He wildly tasted each of them; with joy
> He clutched the gleam of bubbles in the air;
> Without a thought he dropped the dearest heart
> To catch an ugly lewdly painted mask;
> Above all he was called the slave of life,
> Could not grow older, and—was your father!"

Like all of Hofmannsthal's later game-players, Weiden-stamm played the game for keeps and, win or lose, played with all his heart.

The Adventurer and the Singer is unique among Hofmannsthal's works in that it features a variation on the confrontation with self, in which the principal meets two alternate versions of himself. Symbolically, the middle-aged game-player Weidenstamm faces himself both as a young and as an old man during the play. In his son Cesarino, he sees himself as he once was. An old stranger, who comes to his gaming table uninvited and tremblingly wagers the last of his money, could, so Weidenstamm thinks, be his father whom he never knew. In a sense this possibility mirrors his own future. The two encounters thus serve to make of the game of life a fully developed manifestation of the search for identity.

Cristina's Trip Home, a somewhat more light-hearted approach to the man who plays with life, focuses on a question left unanswered by *The Adventurer and the Singer*. It may be argued concerning the latter play that Vittoria achieves personal fulfillment only in marriage.

Until she marries Venier, she really has no life of her own but exists only as a plaything. Hofmannsthal viewed marriage as an integral part of life and was intrigued by the problem of how the adventurer's mistress could become a happily married woman. He assumed that such would be possible only if serving as a plaything were to cause a concrete change in her. In order to demonstrate this point, he created Cristina and made her Florindo-Casanova's innocent victim.

After three unsuccessful weeks in Venice looking for a husband, Cristina meets Florindo as she is leaving with her uncle to go home to the village of Capodiponte. When he is unable to get her to stay in Venice, Florindo impulsively goes along with her. In an inn where they stop to await a wagon that has been sent for them, Florindo seduces Cristina and promises to marry her and give up his reckless ways. Pasca, Cristina's governess, discovers what has taken place and insists that Florindo return to Venice and obtain permission from the archbishop for a wedding. Florindo agrees and leaves Cristina in the company of the retired sea captain Tomaso, who is traveling in the same direction, and who is looking for a wife. Not surprisingly, Florindo falls in love with someone else on the way back to Venice and does not return. Eventually, after overcoming a certain hesitancy on Cristina's part, Tomaso succeeds in winning her for himself. Cristina thus becomes happy in marriage to a dependable man.

It is important to understand that Cristina participates in the experience with Florindo voluntarily, and that Florindo, at least for the moment, appears sincere in his proposal of marriage. Florindo does not intentionally deceive her. Neither does he hide his true nature from her. On the contrary, he confesses openly: "You are a rich heiress and I come to you with nothing. Do you know what I am? An idler. A scoundrel. A gambler." The knowledge of his true character then makes it easier

for Cristina to overcome her disappointment when Florindo does not come back.

The encounter with Florindo brings about a major
change in Cristina herself. She becomes a woman. Specifically, she discovers both her own identity and that of
the kindly Tomaso. In her own words: "Now I know
what a man is and also what a woman is, in God's name."

Cristina's initial reluctance to respond favorably to
Tomaso's advances may be interpreted not as bitterness,
but as the last trace of her old self, which hangs on
without her knowing why. Hofmannsthal expressed it this
way: "Cristina would like simply to say *yes* . . . but
something within her, something both shallow and deep,
both superficial and primitively female says no without a
formulated reason."[4] Once that final echo of the old
Cristina dies away, however, she can make the decision
that brings her the happiness for which she was searching.

As originally written, the play does have one important dramatic flaw, an extremely weak fifth act. The
substance of the act is little more than Cristina's final
acceptance of Tomaso's proposal and a brief visit from
Florindo, who passes by with his new mistress. For the
Berlin premiere in 1910, Max Reinhardt overcame the
problem by omitting the fifth act entirely and dividing the
fourth act into two. In that form the play ultimately became quite popular. Hofmannsthal himself was especially
pleased with "the complete, undisputed, very well noticed
success" of *Cristina* in his own "difficult, hostile Vienna."[5]

Hofmannsthal saw every player of the game of life
as a gambler at heart. For that reason, he consistently
framed dramatic situations in the paraphernalia of games
of chance and symbolically laid bare the souls of his
players by having them place their masks at stake. For
example, at one point in *The Adventurer and the Singer*
Weidenstamm refers to the winnings of an otherwise

poverty-stricken young man as "the mask, the larva of a great man."

Often, however, Hofmannsthal decided that one particular game was more suited than others for a given special effect or to represent a certain kind of interpersonal relationship. In such instances he frequently selected games other than those most overtly associated with gambling. Usually the choice was a game in which skill, judgment, and expertise are more important than the mere element of chance. Appropriate examples include chess, bridge, and billiards.

Chess appears in Hofmannsthal's plays as a background symbol for interchange between characters on stage.[6] A good illustration is a scene in the fragmentary comedy *Sylvia in the Star*. The plot, as far as Hofmannsthal developed it, has the Baron attempting to expose Sylvia as a golddigger. In order to accomplish his purpose, he manipulates other people. That point is brought forcefully home as he plays chess with his secretary. The most obvious instance involves the maid Laroche, whom the Baron hopes to use in his scheme. Just as she walks into the room near where the two are playing, the Baron picks up a piece from the board and says: "Aha, the old rook makes itself useful. Yes, such a ruin can be worth something." Other allusions to chess occur in a fragment entitled "Florindo and the Unknown Woman" and in *Cristina's Trip Home*.

Bridge has a somewhat different function in Hofmannsthal's dramas. Rather than underscore how dominant characters manipulate others, this game illuminates the reactions of the characters to other people and to specific situations. In *The Difficult Man* the primary social activity at the Altenwyl party is the playing of bridge.[7] The card game becomes a metaphor for the various attempts to outwit, second-guess, and relate one to another. Indeed, some figures are even conditioned in their approach to others by what happens when they play cards.

The following situation can be viewed as a typical example: During the party minor characters discuss and interpret the actions of the principal figures. At one point, Antoinette Hechingen converses with three of her friends about her attempts to win back Hans Karl. She asks them for advice. One of them observes that since Antoinette sent her maid to Hans Karl's house only an hour ago, she cannot now play the proud woman. Another disagrees and bases her position on her experience with cards: "I say just the opposite. She must act as if he didn't matter to her. I know this from playing cards: if you take the cards carelessly in your hand, then you get lucky."

What Antoinette's friend fails to recognize is that Hans Karl refuses to play the game of life according to the normal patterns. He is, as Crescence puts it, "a spoil-sport," and as such is no more subject to the bridge-game approach than to the game of hide-and-seek that another woman expects him to play. In fact, one possible interpretation of the entire play is that the greatest "difficulty" with "the difficult man" lies in the fact that he is a non-player in a world of game-players. Ironically, that is what makes him a fitting match for Helene Altenwyl. As he phrases it in one of his comments to her: "After all, neither of us plays."

One truly delightful Hofmannsthal game-player is Theodor, the title figure of *Der Unbestechliche* (The Incorruptible Man). He is alone among Hofmannsthal's heroes in viewing life as a game of billiards. He sees himself as a player at the billiard table, and the various people around him as the billiard balls, whose directions, interactions, and destinies he controls with skillfully executed strokes of his cue.

In the drama, Theodor's opponent is Jaromir, a Florindo type whose mother is an Austrian baroness. At one time Theodor was Jaromir's personal servant. Because he was unable to tolerate Jaromir's life style, he left Jaromir's service and was hired as the baroness's major-domo. Jaromir has recently married and brought his young wife, Anna, to live at his mother's estate. Unfortunately, he is unwilling to break the ties with his former existence and has invited two of his mistresses for a visit. When the baroness refuses to allow Theodor to do anything about the blatant betrayal of Anna, Theodor tenders his resignation.

As the play opens, the baroness has come to realize that she cannot get along without Theodor's help in managing the other servants. The two former mistresses are about to arrive, and everything is in confusion. Backed into a corner, the baroness is forced to give Theodor a free hand. Gleefully he sets to work to upset Jaromir's plans and send Marie and Melanie packing.

His thorough acquaintance with the two women tells him precisely how to handle each of them. As he explains his approach to the baroness, he likens his plan to two different billiard shots.

THEODOR: . . . That one there (*He points to the door through which Marie has just left*) is an unhappy creature with a beautiful, fearful soul. I shall begin to play that one directly. I'll play the other woman off the cushion.

BARONESS: Off the cushion? What does that mean?

THEODOR: Those are expressions borrowed from the game of billiards. I thought they were generally familiar. Melanie, like most women, is stupid and clever at the same time. Accordingly, I said that one must begin to play her indirectly or off the cushion. . . .

Theodor plays Marie "directly" by appealing to her sense of guilt at having left her father alone. She quickly becomes convinced that she should leave.

The off-the-cushion shot is more subtle. By planting appropriate material, Theodor exposes to Melanie the fact that she has become a character in an autobiographical novel that Jaromir is writing. Theodor then reminds Melanie what will happen if her cousins see Jaromir's book. After that, he has no difficulty in persuading her to flee with the manuscript.

In the meantime, Anna has confessed her jealousy of the two women to Jaromir, and he has come to his senses. He promises never to be unfaithful again, thereby bringing Theodor's game to its happy conclusion.

Like all games, the game of life has winners and losers. An impetuous figure like Florindo, who follows the immediate dictates of his emotions, is a sometime winner. Although his winnings are meager and temporary at best, his lot is not especially tragic because he does not really take the game seriously. He is therefore something of a middle thing between the hopeless loser and the unbeatable winner.

In Hofmannsthal's dramas, both the hopeless loser and the unbeatable winner appear less frequently than the Florindo types. Nevertheless, some of Hofmannsthal's most memorable characters are the out-and-out types—either winner or loser.

The hopeless loser is a peculiar kind of tragic hero. He plays the game knowing both what he risks and that he will lose. Yet he is a compulsive gambler and cannot step back from the gaming table. One of the best examples of this type figure is Jaffier, the ne'er-do-well revolutionist in Hofmannsthal's five-act tragedy *Das gerettete Venedig* (Venice Preserved).

Robbed of his dignity by Senator Priuli, who refuses to accept him as his son-in-law, Jaffier agrees to join his friend Pierre in a revolt. The other conspirators demand a sign of his good faith, and he gives them Belvidera, his wife, as hostage. When Belvidera is molested by one of her captors, Jaffier betrays the conspiracy and is quietly executed. All the tragedy of his situation is caught in one brief exchange with his wife. When she tells him that the uprising will fail, he responds:

>   "You know that too?
> That they are the stronger? I've known it all along—
> I have it ceaselessly within me. I play,
> Play ever higher, higher! Now tonight
> I wagered you, then bet away my head
> And knew without the slightest doubt that I
> Could never win."

In contrast, the true winner cannot be defeated because he plays the game knowing that he is in complete control. He is the totally rational player who analyzes every move, seldom makes a mistake, knows his opponents, the stakes, and every fine point of the game. He is a man like Theodor, who understands the game of life for what it is and plays accordingly.

6

Life Is a Dream

In a significant diary entry of June, 1894, Hofmannsthal wrote: "Some people comprehend life through love, others by reflection; I, perhaps, through dreams."[1] For the young Hofmannsthal, the relationship between dream and reality gave rise to an extremely important complex of problems. The preoccupation with dream phenomena had a strong impact on even his earliest creative works.

Hofmannsthal was stimulated in his thinking by Freud's work on the psychology of dreams. In later years, his regard for Freud became so great that in 1924 he made this prediction: "During the course of the century, Freud will be infinitely more powerful than anything that appeared so deeply entrenched around us in our childhood."[2]

Although the dream appears in numerous variations as a metaphor for life in Hofmannsthal's poetry, the major document of the early development of the metaphor is *Das Bergwerk zu Falun* (The Mine at Falun), his first five-act drama.

The Mine at Falun was written in 1899, but was not published in its entirety until after Hofmannsthal's death because he was never satisfied with the play as a whole. He felt that the first act had a unity of its own, and therefore allowed it to be published by itself in 1900. Parts of the remainder of the play appeared piecemeal during the next eleven years. The third act was not pub-

lished at all until 1932, when the complete play came out
in print for the first time. The drama was first staged in
1949.

Like so many of Hofmannsthal's later works, *The
Mine at Falun* was based on material that had already
been treated in literature by earlier writers. In that sense,
the play is an early product of Hofmannsthal's endeavor
to keep alive the substance of European cultural heritage.

In this particular instance, Hofmannsthal modified
and dramatized a story that E. T. A. Hoffmann had written in 1819. Hoffmann, in turn, was one of many authors
in the nineteenth century who wrote literary works dealing with the remarkable events surrounding the recovery
of the body of a miner from a mine at Falun, Sweden.

According to accounts of the actual incident, a
miner named Mats Israëlsson went down alone in a lift-
cage and lost his life in the Mardskins mine in 1670. Fifty
years later, his body was discovered perfectly preserved
in vitriolated water. Nobody recognized him or knew who
he was until an old woman hobbled up on crutches and
identified him as her fiancé, who had perished shortly
before their wedding day.[3]

Hoffmann used these peculiar events as the basis for
his story *The Mine at Falun*, which recounts the life of
the miner Elis Fröbom. Elis begins as a melancholy seaman. His parents have died, leaving him alone and miserable. While reflecting about his mother's death, Elis
meets the ghost-miner Torbern. He then has a dream
about the magical underground realm of the powerful
queen of the mine. Elis decides to take Torbern's advice
and goes to Falun to become a miner. There he falls in
love with his employer's daughter Ulla. He is troubled,
however, by the feeling that he really belongs with the
queen of the mine. Delusions lead him to think he is
discovering rich veins of ore, when he is really bringing
up worthless stones. On the day of the wedding, he goes
to the mine to fetch a red jewel for Ulla's wedding gift

and dies in a cave-in. Fifty years later, his body is found, and Ulla is reunited with her lost fiancé.

Aside from omitting the reunion scene at the end, Hofmannsthal employed most of the main outline of Hoffmann's narrative in creating his drama. Nevertheless, the two stories are totally different in atmosphere and orientation. This is so primarily because Hofmannsthal's Elis Fröbom bears only superficial resemblance to his counterpart in Hoffmann's tale. Hoffmann's Elis is insane, and his madness is the moving force in the events of the story. Hofmannsthal, on the other hand, placed emphasis on the fact that Elis is a dreamer. Accordingly, it is the dream as a creative force that determines Elis's course and shapes the situation of the drama.

The ability to create an alternate reality in the realm of dream is something that Elis has inherited from his father. In the first act of the play, just after Elis has returned home to find his mother dead, Peter, one of his shipmates, gives this assessment of the father-son relationship:

> "His father was the same,
> A helmsman with the gift of second sight.
> He wandered in the moors and mountain chasms
> When in the flesh he was on board with us."

For his part, Elis is aware that he takes after his father but has had difficulty in coping with the implications of that fact. As he phrases it at one point: "To be my father's son,/That was no child's play." It has been especially hard for him to accept the reality of the dream world. He cannot understand, for example, how his father could face his own death as he did. Three days before the old man was burned to death in his cabin, he had seen himself die in a dream, yet had kept silent about it.

Now that Elis is alone in the world, however, dreams have finally become a determining force in his

own life. Indeed, he recognizes that they are the key to
his very identity. In his own words:

> "I could sit still for hours and hours and stare
> At my two hands and dream of that strange man
> To whom these hands of mine really belong."

Once he opens the way for dreams to guide him in
the search for identity, Elis soon becomes aware that he
belongs to another realm. He first recognizes that fact
when Peter suggests that he is really a mole. Elis immediately finds the thought attractive and says:

> "Yes, Peter,
> That may well be. I think you must be right.
> That's not a bad idea. I would like
> To dig my way into the deep, dark earth.
> If only it could be, I'd relish it,
> Like crawling back into my mother's womb."

Gradually this awakened longing grows into a death wish.
A vision of the realm of the dead opens within him, and
while looking intently at the ground he says:

> "House, open up! Yield to me your threshold:
> A son is knocking! Open wide, deep chamber,
> Where hand in hand and hair entwined in hair
> My father with my mother sleeps. I'm coming!"

It is in answer to this plea that the ghost-miner Torbern appears to Elis. The purpose of Torbern's first visit
is actually twofold. He has come both to show Elis the
way into the magical underground dream realm and to
expose him to knowledge of his true nature. Torbern reveals to Elis what is ahead and gives him identity when
he says of Elis's deepest unconscious desire: "It is: to go
with me/To Falun and to be a miner there." At first
Elis does not understand Torbern. He still thinks of himself as a seaman and therefore asks if Torbern means that
he is to *become* a miner. Torbern's response answers the

question of Elis's identity once and for all. He says: "No one becomes what he is not."

In order to confirm in Elis's mind the validity of the prescribed course, Torbern leads Elis into a more powerful dream experience. While still talking to Torbern, Elis feels himself drawn down into the underground realm itself.

Elis's dream descent into the earth is important for the perspective it lends to the relationship in the play between dream and reality. Specifically, the dream world and conscious mortal existence are presented as equally real alternatives that exist side by side. More important, the suggestion is made that the dream realm, from an absolute point of view, is the more valid of the two.

When Elis first becomes conscious of his surroundings in the subterranean chamber, he thinks that the preceding events are a dream from which he has just awakened. Then his first glimpse of the beautiful queen of the mine makes him uncertain that his initial reaction was correct. He says: "I dream, merely dream that I'm awake." While trying to convince Elis that the current experience is real, the queen of the mine reveals the nature of her realm. The dream kingdom differs from mortality in that it is not bound by the laws of time. It can therefore offer a synthesis of all that mortality has ever offered. The queen says:

> "Look! For you up there time flows past without
> A pause, but unto me the power was given
> To plunge into its silent crystal stream
> Against the current, and to glide toward
> Its holy origins. Don't stare at me
> With unseeing eyes! Can't you understand?
> That age-old yesterday, if I invoke it
> Envelops me, and now becomes today:
> The darkened and the dazzling things are gone
> And things long past begin to bloom and grow."

It is this realm then, that the queen of the mine invites Elis to share with her permanently.

Elis, however, is not yet ready to remain in the underground dream kingdom. This fact is also revealed during part of the dream experience. Elis is confronted with the boy Agmahd, a peculiar inhabitant of the mine-queen's world. Agmahd's nature is such that the individual who sees him, sees him as what is secretly within his own heart. Elis first sees Agmahd as a girl with whom he once had a love affair, then as a friend who drowned. These reflections of his inner longings reveal that ties still exist between him and mortal life. Elis is therefore obliged to leave the underground kingdom and to go through a process of purification, during which he must divest himself of those things that bind him to earth life. Only then can he find his way back to the queen of the mine. To achieve that goal, he must follow Torbern's advice and go to Falun.

Elis's love affair with Anna (Hoffmann's Ulla) is a necessary part of his preparation to return permanently to the dream world. It establishes a bond between Elis and mortal existence, that is at least as strong as the attraction of the realm of the queen of the mine. This insures that when Elis does return to the underground kingdom, he will not go because he is forced to do so, but because he makes a free-will choice between two equally alluring alternatives.

For a time the balance between the influences of the respective worlds is upset in that Elis pays attention only to Anna. In the third act of the play, however, he descends into the mine and has a second major confrontation with the mine-queen's realm. This encounter renews the attraction of that realm for him.

Agmahd appears to him again, this time in the form of Anna. Elis pours out his heart to the apparition before he realizes the truth. The realization that he has said words to Agmahd that he can never say again to Anna makes him aware of the choice that he must make. When he hears the living Anna calling him from the mouth of the mine tunnel, he says:

> "Up there they call, my earthly dreams,
> But here the magician draws me, the glistening one,
> To yonder door, there! there! and here's the key."

The door in his dream, when opened, reveals to him once more the blinding glory of the underground kingdom.

At this point, Elis is found unconscious by Anna and her father and is carried back outside where he must make his choice. It is not an easy choice for him to make. After regaining consciousness, he oscillates between the two alternatives. At one point he even suggests to Anna that they flee together, back to the shore whence he first came. Anna rejects this suggestion and forces Elis to choose at last between her and the mine-queen.

In principle, Elis decides to accept himself for what he is, that is, to accept the identity that he recognizes as his own. He explains it to Anna this way: "But for myself, such is my nature, Anna,/That I cannot remain here on the earth." With these words he acknowledges that he belongs to the absolute dream world of the mine-queen.

The most important aspect of Elis's decision is that it brings him fulfillment. Once the final decision is made, he recognizes that he has chosen well. For that reason, he can say to Anna, as he bids her farewell:

> "I go now.
> I must go now. It is time. Don't stare
> At me so full of horror. I am happy."

The Mine at Falun, with its suggestion of final fulfillment in the world of dream, was but one of Hofmannsthal's major treatments of the problem of coping with the reality that the individual generates from within himself. The view that life is a dream was a leitmotif for much of

Hofmannsthal's early work. Eventually, however, the dream approach to life was given its most important development in Hofmannsthal's last major tragedy, *Der Turm* (The Tower).

In September 1902 Hofmannsthal began to work seriously with material from Calderón's comedy *La vida es sueño*. The seventeenth-century play held an allure for Hofmannsthal that is perhaps best described in a passage from a letter that he wrote to Hermann Bahr in 1904: "In the material that attracts me most right now, in *Life Is a Dream*, it is a matter of descending into the uttermost depths of the uncertain labyrinthian kingdom 'self' and finding there the non-self or the world."[4] Yet during those early years, Hofmannsthal limited himself to preparing a German rendition that followed the original quite closely.

Calderón's play presents the story of Sigismund, the imprisoned son of Basilius, King of Poland. Rosaura, who loves Basilius's nephew Astolf, gets lost in the forest with her servant, Clarin. The two women discover the tower where Sigismund is confined and are captured by the tower watchman, who takes them to the king.

At Basilius's court, Sigismund's confinement is explained. Basilius has kept him locked up because of a prophecy that his son would become a ruthless and terrible despot. Basilius has decided, however, to test Sigismund before turning the kingdom over to Astolf. Sigismund is to be given a sleeping potion, brought to the palace, and installed as ruler. If his behavior proves the prophecy false, he will be allowed to retain the kingdom. If not, he will be returned to the tower.

During the test Sigismund acts as was foretold. He mishandles both Rosaura and Estrella, the king's niece, and threatens Basilius with a knife. Accordingly, once subdued he is taken back to his tower prison.

When he awakens in the tower, Sigismund regards what has happened as a dream and decides that all of life is likewise a dream. Nonetheless, he resolves that if his "dreams" should make him king again he will behave differently.

Circumstances afford him a second chance. Soldiers break into the tower and later establish Sigismund on the throne. This time the prince handles himself in a noble manner. He declines to punish his father, brings Rosaura and Astolf together, and marries Estrella. Thus Sigismund ultimately finds fulfillment when his dream world becomes reality.

The experience of World War I, however, made Hofmannsthal more pessimistic about the possibility of finding such a fulfillment. Although the dream metaphor was still appropriate, life had become a nightmare. Consequently, when he again took up the material of *La vida es sueño* in 1916, Hofmannsthal approached it from a completely different angle. As Rudolf Goldschmit wrote: "He was concerned with the question of how Sigismund would fare in a chaotic world that has forsaken spiritual values, and how he must—there was never any doubt in the poet's mind about that—perish in it."[5]

The first version of *The Tower* was published in parts (in *Neue Deutsche Beiträge* in 1923 and 1925), then independently as a whole, in 1925. The second version, in which Hofmannsthal lightened the first three acts and changed the treatment of Sigismund's revolt and eventual death, appeared in 1927. The two versions premiered on the stage simultaneously on February 4, 1928, in Munich and Hamburg respectively. Our discussion here will be confined to the first version of the play.

Except for the basic situation of Sigismund's imprisonment, test, and return to confinement, Hofmannsthal retained in *The Tower* little of the plot of *La vida es sueño*. Instead, he made of Sigismund a victim who cannot reconcile his internal world with the chaotic forces around him.

In a sense, *The Tower* can be interpreted as a symbolic representation of Hofmannsthal's own "prophetic dream" of the future of his own society. In a letter to Hofmannsthal of October 1921, his friend Carl J. Burckhardt wrote: "Surely this material goes quite beyond your own life. It is the tragedy of a whole world, a world of which you yourself are one of the last representatives."[6]

The Sigismund of Hofmannsthal's play is initially an extremely pathetic figure. His external circumstances are those of a captive animal. He is confined to an open cage in the tower courtyard, clothed only in a pelt. Because he is deprived of conversation with anyone except Anton, his guard, Sigismund's only activity is that of killing the vermin that enter his cage.

His physical deprivation is mild compared to his spiritual suffering. Because of his isolation, he has no concept of where he is or what role he plays in the world outside himself. Thus, when a doctor is sent to examine him, Sigismund asks: "Where have they put me? Am I now in the world? Where is the world?" Until he has the answers to these and other questions that trouble him, he is unable to cope at all with those who manipulate and use him for their own purposes.

Sigismund is Hofmannsthal's symbol for a mankind that is denied its rightful position in an orderly world. The doctor, whose objective analysis of the situation mediates Hofmannsthal's intent, makes this point clear when he says of Sigismund's situation: "This horrible crime has been committed against the whole of humanity." In this light, the tower itself symbolizes the reality to which man is confined without hope of escape.

The body of the drama documents Sigismund's development of a perception of his own identity. The major difficulty that he encounters in the process is that it is often impossible to distinguish between external and internal reality, between life and dream. Hermann Broch captured with great precision the essence of Sigismund's problem when he wrote: "Again and again dream and life merge; again and again the merging is impenetrable temptation. More and more, it is necessary to hang on to the dream in order to be able to hang on to life. And with that necessity there is always the danger that life will turn into dream."[7]

The principal event in Sigismund's awakening to personal awareness is his return to Basilius's court, his "dream" excursion into the real world. The circumstances leading up to this experience are somewhat different in *The Tower* from those in *La vida es sueño*.

While the doctor is visiting Sigismund, Julian, the commander of the tower prison, is summoned to Basilius. The king's nephew has died, leaving the king without an heir. Sensing an opportunity to gain power for himself, Julian develops a plan to put Sigismund on the throne. He suggests that Sigismund be brought to the court and observed to see if his actions confirm the prediction.

Julian's defense of his plan reveals the framework into which Sigismund's experience will fall: We read:

JULIAN: If he did not pass the test, one would let him disappear again into the night of his dungeon. To that wretched person it would be like the short dream of a heavy sleep.

KING: A night's dream? Bold—but too bold!

JULIAN: (*quickly*): Not too bold! Through action the world becomes the world for us. He has never acted; he knows only shadows and pictures, only dreams!

The implications of Julian's thinking are clear. Because of his isolation, Sigismund knows only the world that he has created within himself. Because of his lack of experience, he can be readily returned to that world if necessary, without his really understanding what has taken place.

Because of his feelings of guilt concerning the confining of his son, Basilius agrees to the plan, and Julian returns to the tower to get Sigismund.

In the scene that describes the preparations for
Sigismund's journey, Hofmannsthal underscores once
more the contrast between Sigismund's perception of the
world and what he is about to experience. To Sigismund,
the world is really a vast unknown. The things that he has
projected from within himself are incomplete. He tells
Anton, for example, that he saw his father in a fire that
he started in the straw of his bed. When Anton asks what
his father looked like, Sigismund responds: "My father
has no face."

More important, Sigismund is troubled now more
than ever by the question of his own identity. When Julian tells him that he must take the sleeping potion, he is
afraid of being poisoned. Yet so important to him is the
question of his identity that he says: "You taught me that
they poison prisoners with a drink. But tell me first who I
am, and I will follow you like a lamb."

In a way, what takes place just before Sigismund
leaves for the palace is more important for his dawning
awareness of himself than is the palace experience itself.
The sleeping potion enables him to have a vision that
reveals to him the essence of his internal world, and to
recognize the natural unity that exists between him and
the outside world. He describes his personal revelation in
these words:

"A man may believe that he does evil or good to his fellow
man, but who touches what is inside him? That is untouch-
able. I lamented that my father was hidden. My father is
within me. It is difficult for a man to recognize what is near
him. He sees the walls but doesn't see who is in the room
with him. In here (*he folds his arms across his chest*) are
the four ends of the earth. Faster than an eagle I fly from
one to the other, and yet I am in one piece and as dense as
ebony. That is the secret."

Yet in the real world, Sigismund cannot cope with
the answers he receives to the questions about his origins

and identity. When he arrives at the palace, he is unable to reconcile with his past experiences the ideas of having a living father and a role in the real world. He seizes his real-world identity and attempts to assert his power, thereby becoming indeed the predicted tyrant. As a result, he is subdued and taken back to the tower, where he reenters his inner world, convinced that the world of dream is the only true reality.

There is a certain irony in the backfiring of Julian's plan. In the fourth act of the play, Julian comes to the tower to persuade Sigismund to join him in revolt against Basilius. Sigismund refuses, saying that the outside world is only a dream. Because his ruse has worked so well, Julian now finds it impossible to convince Sigismund otherwise.

When the soldier Olivier betrays Julian and takes over the revolt, he too tries to force Sigismund to take part. He is equally unsuccessful. Sigismund continues to insist that there is only one truth: "We know of nothing as it really is, and there is nothing of which we could say that it is of a nature different from our dreams."

For Sigismund, the dream has become a creative force. He refuses to join either Julian or Olivier because their course is one of destruction. When the common people come, however, and beg him to be their king, he joins them so as to put down the revolt and establish a new order that corresponds to the projections of his inner world. Unfortunately, to achieve this end, Sigismund must reenter the real world.

While Sigismund's forces are pursuing the rebel Olivier, they capture Olivier's mistress and bring her to Sigismund. Unknown to the latter, Olivier is already dead and his mistress has come looking for revenge. As she cowers before Sigismund in his tent, she mediates a vision in which the dead Olivier, Julian, and Basilius appear. Sigismund is so caught up in what he seems to see, that he does not notice when the woman cuts him across the hand with a poisoned knife. Ironically, his destruction comes about because he remains dominated in the world of reality by the dream realm within him.

Sigismund's death, however, means only that the new order will be guided by a different king, the mysterious King of the Children who comes to the dying Sigismund, hallows his death, and declares an end to the acts of violence that destroyed the old order. The arrival of the King of the Children gives the last act of *The Tower* an apocalyptic quality reminiscent of the Revelation of St. John. It suggests that although the dreamer himself is doomed to perish in the chaos of the modern world, there may still be hope that the dream of life will end in fulfillment after all.

7

Life Is a Poem

The spring wind is gliding
Mid boughs that are bare,
In his heart hiding
Strange things and rare.[1]

These opening lines from "Early Spring" do more than simply introduce one of Hofmannsthal's earliest poems. In a real sense they also describe his entry into the German literary world. In the literary climate of the 1890s, Hugo von Hofmannsthal the lyric poet was indeed a "spring wind" with "strange things" hiding in his heart. In reality, he was an enigma to his contemporaries.

It was not that his poetry lacked roots in tradition. On the contrary, his verse depended on ideas and prosody drawn from a broad range of models. An obvious example is the third of his "Stanzas in Terza Rima." The whole poem is an elaboration of the first line, which in turn is essentially a literal translation of Prospero's words in Shakespeare's *The Tempest*, "We are such stuff as dreams are made of."

Nor did the young poet stand outside the literary currents of his own generation. Like his friends, Hermann Bahr, Arthur Schnitzler, and Richard Beer-Hofmann, Hofmannsthal was an impressionist.

Literary impressionism, of course, demanded the faithful reproduction of subjective sensual impression and

precisely observed mood. Its proponents were acutely
conscious of the incidental, the transitory, the unique
spiritual state in all its finest differentiations, nuances,
halftones, and hues. They sought to accomplish their
purposes through the greatest possible perfection and
purification of literary language and form of expression.

Hofmannsthal's lyric creations meet these criteria in
every respect. His treatment of visual themes is especially
effective. As one of his contemporaries worded it, Hofmannsthal possessed to a high degree of refinement "the
ability to observe nature and life through the eyes of a
great painter and to create in that style."[2] Albrecht
Schaeffer expresses essentially the same idea when he
says: "Thus Hofmannsthal is, in conformity with the
artistic perception of his time, a combiner of spiritual
with sensual sight, an impressionist of seeing."[3]

The systematic cultivation of a highly elevated literary language was something that concerned Hofmannsthal throughout his life. That was one reason why he was
wooed by Stefan George. George saw perfection of literary expression as the essence of poetry. He would hardly
have courted Hofmannsthal so persistently, had it not
been for the power that informed his language. In a
couplet entitled "Personal Language," Hofmannsthal
caught the substance of his own infatuation with the awe-
some power of words. He wrote this distich:

> As language has grown in your mouth, the chain
>   in your hand has been strengthened;
> Pull the universe to you! Pull now!
>   Or you'll be dragged.[4]

Obviously then, in point of approach at least, Hofmannsthal's poetry did fit the demands of the last years of
the nineteenth century. What made his verses so extraordinary was the supreme mastery of poetic technique
that they exhibited from the beginning. Not since Goethe
had any German poet been so skillful.

The fact that Hofmannsthal appeared on the literary scene as an accomplished poet rather than a "beginner" caused considerable speculation as to his destiny. Usually, enduring success is based on a long process of artistic maturation. As a result, critics were inclined to predict a short, flashy career. Josef Hofmiller, for example, warned of the danger inherent in Hofmannsthal's obvious reliance on the vast European literary tradition. He saw Hofmannsthal imperiled by the overly precious elements of that heritage.[5]

In the sense that Hofmannsthal's career as a lyric poet was relatively brief, the prophecies of such skeptics were perspicacious. Nevertheless, in those few short years, Hofmannsthal contributed to German literature poems of lasting beauty that outshine the total oeuvre of many poets.

What Hofmannsthal accomplished in his so-called "lyric decade" was to capsulize in verse, while still a young man, the various aspects of his approach to life. Although he later expanded, and in many instances refined, the embryonic ideas contained in his poems in his prose narratives, dramas, and opera librettos, he never expressed a more complete picture of his entire world view than he did in his poetry.

It should also be pointed out in passing, that Hofmannsthal had another major poetic achievement during this period. His experiments with verse led him to the short lyric play. Prior to his early attempts, that genre was virtually nonexistent in the literature of the German-speaking countries. Hofmannsthal can therefore be credited with making the one-act verse drama a part of German literature.

Upon close examination, Hofmannsthal's poems can be accurately described as a combination of vision and interpretation of the world and its phenomena. They pertain to the present and to both the future and the past. In

Hofmannsthal's poetic world, past, present, and future
are inseparable.

One basic human experience in which present, past,
and future are brought together in an eternal now is death.
In the blank-verse poem, "An Experience," written in
1892, Hofmannsthal gave an extremely beautiful rendering of his views on death.[6] His ideas are presented in a
series of reflections generated by impressions of a dark
valley. The first few lines of the poem describe how
Hofmannsthal's thoughts mingled with the atmosphere of
the valley and how he subsequently "drowned in the
translucent,/Light-weaving ocean" of that atmosphere
and "left life behind." There follows a flood of vivid
sense impressions, particularly of color and sound. Soon
the poet is able to give the experience a name: "This
must be death."

That recognition is followed by an immediate longing for the life that has been lost. The longing is compared to that of a person on a ship, sailing past his home
town, unable to cross to the land that symbolizes his own
childhood.

"An Experience" is but one of several poems that
are best interpreted in terms of the concept that Hofmannsthal called "preexistence." According to his development of this idea, existence has two points of reference. Mortal life is one point, preexistence the other. It
follows that preexistence is man's state when he is "outside" mortal life. It is where he comes from when he is
born, where he goes at death, and where he is when
momentarily apart from conscious life in dreams or other
such experiences. In this framework, preexistence is absolute existence, while mortality is a temporary state that
has very little meaning without reference to preexistence.

Hofmannsthal's clearest portrayal of the emptiness
of a world devoid of the acceptance of preexistence is
found in his "Ballad of the Outer Life." The poem ques-

tions the relevance of mortal existence and emphasizes the transitoriness of all things earthly. The material things of this poem's world, because of their very lack of coherence, of connections to things beyond themselves, cannot possibly have enduring value. Likewise, man's experiences of laughter, tears, and death, are meaningless because man wanders aimlessly and does not see beyond the present and himself.

There is, however, an alternative for the individual who is conscious of preexistence. Hofmannsthal discusses that alternative in three poems entitled collectively "Stanzas in Terza Rima." These poems too treat the problem of transitoriness, but place man's existence in an entirely different perspective.

The first of the "Stanzas in Terza Rima" has something of the form of a response to "Ballad of the Outer Life":

I

On Transitoriness

Her breath, I feel it still upon my face:
How can it be that these near days are borne
Away, forever lost without a trace?

This is what none can fully comprehend,
And much too terrible for us to mourn,
That everything glides by, flows to an end.

And that my very self, by nothing bound
Could flow across and from a child descend,
To me, like some strange dog that makes no sound.

That I a hundred years ago was there,
That my ancestors, lying in the ground,
Are as akin to me as my own hair.

As much a part of me as my own hair.[7]

The important thing about "Terza Rima I" is its question as to whether the past can really be "borne

away, forever lost without a trace." To the realization
that the poet's own essence proceeded forth "from a
child," is added the haunting consciousness that he existed before the child did, and that therefore his experience is not without contact with what lies beyond. Quite
the contrary. Identifiable beings in the preexistence, his
own dead ancestors, are as much a living part of him as
his own hair.

Death itself and its consequences also gain a different illumination in the light of preexistence. The second
of the "Stanzas in Terza Rima" is a treatment of death.

II

The hours! When we gaze out into the blue
Of ocean waves and grasp death's meaning there,
All horror gone, a light yet solemn view,

Like little girls who look so pale and fair
With their enormous eyes, who always freeze,
And in the evening mutely stand and stare,

And recognize that life now softly flees
From sleepy limbs to trees and grassy bed,
And smile affected smiles with weary ease

Like persecuted saints whose blood is shed.[8]

In this poem—which is, by the way, quite characteristic of Hofmannsthal's approach to human mortality—
death is not a feared unknown. Rather, it is something
that the poet understands. Actually there is no such thing
as death, but only the flow of life from one form to
another.

In Hofmannsthal's system, there are two aspects to
the change that occurs at death. In the poem "An Experience" he portrayed the transition of the individual
from mortality to preexistence in the death experience. In
stanzas in "Terza Rima II" he points to the transfer of
life energy from one entity to another in the image of life
flowing from pale little girls into trees and grass.

This too is in harmony with the concept of preexistence and its relationship to mortality. Hofmannsthal regarded the absolute progress of the individual as following a course leading repeatedly from life to preexistence and back again through a sequence of different life forms. This idea is presented most clearly in the following lines from "Ghazel II," a poem written in 1891 that compares the development of the poet with that of the individual soul:

> Every living spirit wanders through the hierarchy
>   of beings,
> Changing, purifying forms, becoming happy, greater,
>   brighter,
> On it lives in worm, in frog, in vampire bat, in
>   lowly slave,
> Then in dancer, in poet, vagabond, and noble
>   fighter.[9]

Obviously the process of transformation is one of purification. Yet the direction is not always upward. The transition may be from worm to frog, or from poet to vagabond.

As he grappled again and again with problems inherent in the transient nature of life, there emerged in Hofmannsthal's works three major metaphors for the mortal state: the dream, the drama, and the game. All of these are experiences or situations of brief duration. At the same time, the course of each is subject to infinite variety. To be sure, Hofmannsthal did not invent the metaphors. They are but one more sign of the intensity of the bond between him and European literary tradition. As we have seen, the metaphors came into full flower in Hofmannsthal's longer literary forms, especially the dramas. Yet they appear in considerable variation in his verse.

The dream metaphor represents life as a process occurring totally within the individual. "Stanzas in Terza

Rima III" is the first of Hofmannsthal's poems to place
specific emphasis on that internal focus.

III

> The stuff of which we're made has properties
> Like that of dreams, and dreams open their eyes
> Like little children under cherry-trees,
>
> Out of whose crowns the full moon's path does rise
> All pale and golden lit through the great night.
> . . . Our dreams develop in this selfsame wise,
>
> Are there, a laughing child, alive and bright,
> No less significant in ebb and flow
> Than, rising o'er the trees, the full moon's light.
>
> Our inmost thoughts pervade their to and fro.
> Like ghost hands locked in some small room, they
>   gleam,
> They are in us and always have life's glow.
>
> And three are one: a man, a thing, a dream.[10]

The key idea here is that dreams are a creative
force. More important is what they help create: the identity of the individual. Because "the stuff of which we're
made has properties like that of dreams," we merge with
our dreams and, as the last line indicates, become one
with them.

Just as dreams themselves vary, so Hofmannsthal
offers a number of variations on the life-is-a-dream motif
in his poems. "The Old Man's Longing for the Summer,"
for example, emphasizes the idea that the most valid
world is the one we dream of.[11] This particular poem
gives a good illustration of the subtlety with which Hofmannsthal employed language. As the old man projects
himself ever further into the dream of summer, a transformation of the poem's language takes place. In the first
five stanzas the old man hypothesizes what he would do if
it were summer. In the German original this is signaled

by the use of the subjunctive mood in the verbs. Beginning with the sixth stanza, however, the descriptions are
offered in the indicative. As the old man becomes one
with what he envisions, his verbal portrait no longer represents hypothesis, but personal inner reality. Indeed,
three stanzas from the end, this inner reality merges with
external reality when the old man refers once more to the
reality of March as a shadow upon "the moonlit sum-
mery land."

Significantly, the thing that impresses the old man
most about the experience is that the dream world generates no doubts for him. Unlike physical reality, there is
nothing here that whispers: "All this is nothing," no nag-
ging uncertainty to suggest that "this is vain."

The idea that existence is a unified whole, and that
the individual is the nucleus of that whole is extremely
important to Hofmannsthal's system of thought. The individual is the center, because everything outside him, in
the sense that it exists only as he perceives it, is his
creation. Yet at the same time that created unity exists
only within him. In order to carry out his responsibility to
the world, the person must "feel" the existing interde-
pendence. The dream is one device that enables him to
do so.

As employed by Hofmannsthal, the second major
metaphor, "life is a drama," is also a direct outgrowth of
the preexistence concept. Because an entity progresses by
passing through a series of external identities, he becomes
like an actor playing a different role each time he comes
on stage. Hofmannsthal also liked the metaphor for another reason. By nature he was a spectator. In viewing
life as theater he could place himself in the audience at
will. From the perspective of a spectator, Hofmannsthal
wrote those poems that presented the drama metaphor
most powerfully.

One of the most famous of these is "Prologue to
'Anatol,'" which was written to honor a work by Hof-

mannsthal's friend Arthur Schnitzler.[12] The poem begins
with an overwhelming, almost haphazard, heterogeneous
series of impressions taken from the realm of the stage.
Railings, hedges, coats of arms, sphinxes, squeaking
gates, and waterfalls appear in jumbled array. Throughout the first part of the poem properties and scenery are
mixed with snatches of scenes, seemingly unrelated actors, and bits and pieces of color and atmosphere. The
result is a vibrant mosaic of elements connected only by
their common association with the theater.

In the second section of the poem, we are given the
reasons for the apparent confusion. The theater represents the broad diversity of life. The plays that are staged
are spontaneous, generated from within the actors themselves. The poet broadens the metaphor to include himself and the reader among the players and summarizes
their participation by describing life as "plays that we
have fashioned" and "comedies of our own spirit." In so
doing, Hofmannsthal gives his own rendering of Shakespeare's "All the world's a stage," that famous utterance
of Jacques from *As You Like It*.

Another kind of spectator poem that Hofmannsthal
wrote was the elegy, a number of which are dedicated to
the memory of real persons. The elegies concern themselves more with a single aspect of the drama metaphor,
the actor as symbolic man. The poem "In Memory of the
Actor Mitterwurzer" is quite typical of Hofmannsthal's
treatment of this theme.[13]

At the death of the actor there is immediate awareness that something special has died. With him have perished all the characters to whom he gave life. The characters are dead because the special life that this actor gave
them was unique and could come only from him. Though
another actor would play the same role, the life thus
given would somehow be different, and the character,
despite the mask and properties, would be a new one. It
is the feeling of permanent loss that prompts the poet to

ask concerning Mitterwurzer: "But just who was he, and who was he not?"

The answer to the question is interesting but not surprising. In essence the dead actor is identical with the dreamer. He is the creator and center of existence. Moreover, as with the dreamer, the world he creates comes from inside himself. Hofmannsthal describes Mitterwurzer's body as "a magic veil" in which everything dwells, a veil from which the actor was capable of drawing not only assorted animals and people, but also, and perhaps most important, "you and me."

In short, the actor possesses the power to give life. In Hofmannsthal's scheme this makes him a vehicle in which individuals can cross over from preexistence to mortality. By the death of Mitterwurzer such a vehicle has been lost. The great tragedy is therefore not the death of characters already portrayed but the loss of things yet to come. The essence of the final lament of the poem is that the actor's death has caused figures from our own internal world to depart, and has precluded others who might have been born within us from ever coming.

Life viewed as a game is the least well developed of the metaphors in the poetry. Hofmannsthal later dealt largely with adult games, with gambling and the figure of the adventurer as a player of games. He apparently found the gambler type somewhat unsuited for the limited scope of a poem. In his lyric poems, the game imagery is primarily that of the child's game.

In Hofmannsthal's usage the game emerges as an aspect of the created world of the individual. While forming his world, the person "teaches" its inhabitants games. The games then characterize people within the created world. One illustration of this relationship is found in the first part of "The Youth and the Spider."[14] While speaking of the world as he sees it, the young man of the poem reveals himself as a typical Hofmannsthal figure, conscious of his position at the center of a universe, of which the decrees of fate have made him ruler. While surveying his "subjects," he notes their relationship to him. Many who dwell in his internal world have his own features. More important, they play games that he as their creator has taught them.

On occasion, Hofmannsthal depicts his player of games as having special strength as an individual. In the long poem "A Prologue," Hofmannsthal employs the image of a table at which places are set only for victors. In the present context the following lines are especially interesting:

> There is a chair and dish for each of those
> Who fought and overcame great muffled powers:
> And one ballplayer, I have heard, was chosen,
> The one most elegant, and yet the strongest
> To whom no player ever hit a ball back,
> No, not the biggest. Yet he played while smiling,
> As though he merely knocked the tops from flowers.[15]

The strong man plays the game of life to win. Obviously, however, there is always the risk of losing. To Hofmannsthal, this was the most important aspect of the game. There is really little meaning in playing unless something important is at stake. In his later works the willingness, indeed the compulsion, to take chances is the outstanding characteristic of man, the game player. As we have seen in an earlier chapter, the gambler was to become Hofmannsthal's embodiment of the unfulfilled life.

Given Hofmannsthal's three symbols for man— dreamer, actor, player—one may reasonably ask: Which of these was he? Undoubtedly, he saw himself as a synthesis of all of them, a synthesis that he called "poet." The poet, after all, is the ultimate creator. As Hofmannsthal saw it, the poet accomplishes what none of the others can. He causes people to become creators in their own right, helps them find the worlds locked within themselves. Hofmannsthal's view of his own role is set down in this famous poem:

Where I Near and Where I Land . . .

Where I near and where I land,
Here in shadow, there in sand
They all take their places near me;
I give joy to those who hear me,
Bind them with the shadow-band.

From known things that illustrate them
I teach secrets that await them:
How their limbs move low and high,
Motions in the starry sky,
They can scarcely separate them.

For I tell them: "One great might
Guides the day and ends the night,
But within you deeply buried
Highly secret realms are carried
Quiet, hidden, out of sight."

Then they stare with pent-up dread
At themselves where eyes are lead,
By the secret permeated,
Feel themselves now elevated,
Dark sky bluer overhead.[16]

This poem is a powerful example of depth in simplicity. It describes the rapport the poet would like to have with his public. Basically, what is desired is the relationship of teacher to student. Yet what is taught and the manner of teaching cause the communication to go much deeper. On the basis of symbols they understand, the poet acquaints his disciples with the mysteries of their connection to the whole. Then he unfolds the great secret of their own internal mysteries, and the listeners focus inward upon themselves. That was the goal of Hofmannsthal's poetry, to awaken people to their own potential, so that, permeated by the secret, they could feel themselves uplifted.

Hofmannsthal apparently felt that many of his poems failed to accomplish his intent. When Stefan George urged him to publish a collection in 1897, he responded: "You will approve of my not collecting my verses, when you consider that all in all I cannot bring together twenty-five poems that I would want to have included in a book."[17] Fortunately, he eventually changed his mind.

8

Synthesis

In 1907, Hofmannsthal published an essay entitled "The Poet and This Time." It was based in part on ideas taken from Schiller's *Über die ästhetische Erziehung des Menschen.*[1]

Hofmannsthal's main purpose in writing "The Poet and this Time" was to compare the respective social roles of modern and earlier writers. Using Schiller's time-citizen concept as a point of departure, Hofmannsthal attempted to demonstrate that the role the poet plays depends upon the time in which he lives. He argued that because a poet must be a "living" force to be relevant, the poet must use his genius to convey to the reader the essence of the times. The role of the poet is thus inseparable from the age in which he lives.

It is extremely difficult to assess what the modern poet should be doing. Hofmannsthal argues that since ethical constants are absent, it is impossible to define the poet's role in terms of such constants. Therefore the public fails—whether the poet or his influence is actually in evidence or not—to accord the poet his rightful status of leadership. Indeed, the modern poet has become the antithesis of the leader. Hofmannsthal describes him in these words:

He dwells peculiarly in the house of time, under the stairs where all must pass by him, but where nobody pays attention to him. . . . He dwells unrecognized in his own house, under the stairs, in the dark, with the dogs. He is a stranger and yet at home, a dead man, a phantom that everyone talks about, . . . without rights, without responsibility except to loaf, to lie around, to weigh all of this upon an invisible balance within himself, and to experience tremendous suffering and tremendous joy. . . .

Hofmannsthal attributes the modern public's failure to accept the poet to its inability to distinguish between the poet's role in the present and that of the past. In order to place the poet of the twentieth century in his proper perspective, Hofmannsthal devotes the rest of his essay to reorienting the public toward a realistic view of contemporary poesy.

For Hofmannsthal, the main task of the poet was to provide the reader with an access to the whole of human experience. In speaking of the poet, Hofmannsthal wrote: "In him everything must and will come together. It is he, who within himself binds together the elements of the times. Either the present is within him or it is nowhere." Yet the poet also unites the present with the past to make elements of the past a living and relevant part of the present. He records, preserves, and analyzes everything that moves his time, whether from the present, past, or future. Hofmannsthal refers to him metaphorically as a seismograph vibrating with every tremor. It is not that the poet thinks unceasingly about everything in the world, but rather that everything in the world acts upon him. For him, everything is living reality that affects the present.

The public, however, desires to enjoy the fruits of the poet's intimacy with the times. It therefore expects of the poet a synthesis of the "content" of the times. When this synthesis is not in evidence, the poet loses his leadership. Herein lies the necessity to awaken the public to the difference in the product of the contemporary poet as compared to that of his predecessors.

Hofmannsthal asserted that the works of earlier

poets yield the type of synthesis for which the present-day public is searching. The modern poet, however, does not create such a synthesis. That does not mean that the poet has not fulfilled his responsibilities to the present era. Both the times and the poet's relationship to them have changed. The events of the preceding century have emphasized individual experience so strongly that the focus of interest has shifted away from the composite. The demand for a synthesis no longer fits reality. The world of the new generation is within the self. The responsible poet of the present era must therefore use what he experiences of the times to awaken the reader to the inner world of his own experience.

The poet of the twentieth century, according to Hofmannsthal, has an even greater responsibility than those before him. The former duty to synthesize has been replaced by the duty to awaken the reader to himself, thus enabling the latter to create his own internal synthesis and thereby establish his own "time citizenship."

Hofmannsthal's works as a whole document his life-long attempt to satisfy the stringent demands set forth in "The Poet and this Time." The views expressed in this essay, concerning what literature should be and do, explain in part the immense diversity of Hofmannsthal's creations, and even why he extended his creative efforts into the realm of the opera. A single genre, even a combination of genres, could not by itself convey the essence of Hofmannsthal's era as he felt it should be conveyed. He saw each individual work as exposing the reader to only a small part of human experience and existence. It took many works of many different kinds to even suggest a degree of appreciation for the whole.

In his essays, Hofmannsthal tried to meet his own demand that the poet record, preserve, and analyze everything that moves his time. Among the things that he considered most important in that regard were art, music, literature, theater, architecture, history, politics, religion, philosophy, people, places, cultural institutions, and language. He wrote penetrating, colorful, provocative essays about all of these and more.

Hofmannsthal's poetry represents a very special attempt to give the reader a meaningful sampling of the myriad of possibilities for self-interpretation, to acquaint him with just a few of the things that can be found or created within the individual's internal world. Although the poems too are diverse, they all offer answers to two basic questions: What is man? How can man perceive and thus create himself and that which comprises his personal world?

The prose narratives stress the fact that life is the experience of the individual. Again and again the stories point out the fallacy in being passive, in waiting for others to make life meaningful. No person in Hofmannsthal's literary world can find or establish his personal identity without actively working to create it. In Hofmannsthal's terms, the failure to act is the failure to live.

Hofmannsthal came closest to achieving the personal artistic synthesis that he sought for himself, in his dramas and operas. In writing them he utilized elements from personal experience, history, fantasy, and the writings of others, to create literary works that would have the power to touch the lives of actors and spectators alike. Moreover, through his works for the stage as nowhere else he realized the goal of reawakening the public to the whole of European cultural heritage.

The goal of Hofmannsthal's literary work, then, was to provide the tools, the stimulus, the raw materials that the author deemed necessary for an individual to create, awaken, or expand his internal world and achieve his own personal artistic synthesis. In pursuing that goal, Hofmannsthal also succeeded in creating such a synthesis for himself. Perhaps the best description of that synthesis is given in his own words:

What I have experienced, seen, guessed, or dreamed in life, and what has seemed to me of all those things to be worthy of note as well as beautiful to the inner senses: feelings of loneliness, feelings of love, and feelings of defiance, combined with experiences and situations that richly exude and blend these feelings, woven together with landscapes, specific faces, and other external things, which themselves lend to the situations in mind special attraction and the aroma of special things and experiences—that, taken together, interwoven, is what my works are.[2]

Notes

1. LIFE IS LONELINESS

1. Rudolf Borchardt, "Erinnerungen," in *Hugo von Hofmannsthal*, ed. Helmut A. Fiechtner (Bern and Munich, 1963), p. 83.
2. Hugo von Hofmannsthal and Rudolf Borchardt, *Briefwechsel* (Frankfurt am Main, 1954), p. 65.
3. Edmund von Hellmer, "Hofmannsthal als Gymnasiast," Fiechtner, pp. 34–35.
4. Carl J. Burckhardt, *Erinnerungen an Hofmannsthal* (Munich, 1964), p. 44.
5. Hugo von Hofmannsthal and Edgar Karg von Bebenburg, *Briefwechsel* (Frankfurt am Main, 1966), p. 146.
6. Herman Bahr, "Loris," Fiechtner, p. 40.
7. Bahr, p. 41.
8. Stefan George and Hugo von Hofmannsthal, *Briefwechsel* (Berlin, 1938), p. 13.
9. George and Hofmannsthal, pp. 14–15.
10. George and Hofmannsthal, p. 236.
11. George and Hofmannsthal, p. 58.
12. George and Hofmannsthal, pp. 68–69.
13. Hugo von Hofmannsthal and Carl J. Burckhardt, *Briefwechsel* (Frankfurt am Main, 1956), p. 78.
14. Hofmannsthal and Burckhardt, p. 226.
15. Hofmannsthal and Burckhardt, pp. 233–234.
16. George and Hofmannsthal, p. 117.
17. George and Hofmannsthal, p. 149.
18. George and Hofmannsthal, p. 158.
19. George and Hofmannsthal, p. 227.
20. Hugo von Hofmannsthal and Richard Strauss, *A Working Friendship*, trans. Hanns Hammelmann and Ewald Osers (New York, 1961), p. 18.

21. Hofmannsthal and Strauss, p. 29.
22. Hofmannsthal and Strauss, p. 18.
23. Hofmannsthal and Strauss, p. 42.
24. Hofmannsthal and Strauss, p. 93.
25. Hofmannsthal and Strauss, p. 91.
26. Hofmannsthal and Strauss, p. 144.
27. Hofmannsthal and Strauss, p. 156.
28. Hugo von Hofmannsthal, *Gesammelte Werke in Einzel-ausgaben. Prosa IV* (Frankfurt am Main, 1966), p. 92.
29. Hofmannsthal, *Prosa IV*, p. 91.
30. Frederick Ritter, *Hugo von Hofmannsthal und Öster-reich* (Heidelberg, 1967), p. 11.
31. Hugo von Hofmannsthal, "Briefe an Willy Wiegand und die Bremer Presse," *Jahrbuch der Deutschen Schiller-Gesellschaft* VII (1963) : 73.
32. Carl J. Burckhardt, "Erinnerungen an Hofmannsthal," Fiechtner, p. 130.
33. Hofmannsthal and Strauss, p. 318.
34. Hofmannsthal and Strauss, p. 397.
35. For statistics on performance of Hofmannsthal's works on the German-speaking stage since 1945, see Günther Erken, "Hofmannsthal auf den deutschsprachigen Bühnen seit 1945," *Hofmannsthal Blätter* (1968), Nr. 1, pp. 31–40.
36. Hofmannsthal and Strauss, p. 479.
37. Hofmannsthal and Strauss, p. 380.
38. Hofmannsthal, "Briefe an Willy Wiegand . . . ," p. 131.
39. Hugo von Hofmannsthal and Leopold von Andrian, *Briefwechsel* (Frankfurt am Main, 1968), pp. 393, 437.

2. THE THEORY OF LIFE

1. Elsbeth Pulver, *Hofmannsthals Schriften zur Literatur* (Bern, 1956), p. 22.
2. Hermann Broch, *Hofmannsthal und seine Zeit* (Frankfurt am Main, 1974), p. 92.
3. Donald G. Daviau, "Hugo von Hofmannsthal and the Chandos Letter," *Modern Austrian Literature* 4 (1971) : 28.

4. Hugo von Hofmannsthal and Leopold von Andrian, *Briefwechsel* (Frankfurt am Main, 1968), p. 160.

5. See especially Lowell A. Bangerter, *Schiller and Hofmannsthal* (Madrid, 1974), and Grete Schaeder, *Hugo von Hofmannsthal und Goethe* (Hameln, 1947).

3. THE SEARCH FOR IDENTITY

1. Hugo von Hofmannsthal, *Briefe an Marie Herzfeld* (Heidelberg, 1967), p. 27.

2. Hugo von Hofmannsthal and Arthur Schnitzler, *Briefwechsel* (Frankfurt am Main, 1964), p. 63.

3. Wolfgang Köhler, *Hugo von Hofmannsthal und "Tausendundeine Nacht"* (Bern and Frankfurt am Main, 1972), p. 73.

4. Hofmannsthal and Schnitzler, pp. 63–64.

5. Jakob Laubach, *Hugo von Hofmannsthals Turmdichtungen* (Kempten, 1954), p. 14.

6. Köhler, p. 81.

7. Uwe Böker, "Hugo von Hofmannsthals Märchen der 672. Nacht," *Archiv* 206 (1969/70) : 22.

8. Richard Alewyn, *Über Hugo von Hofmannsthal* (Göttingen, 1967), p. 80.

9. Volker O. Durr, "Der Tod des Wachtmeisters Anton Lerch und die Revolution von 1848: Zu Hofmannsthals *Reitergeschichte*," *German Quarterly* 45 (1972) : 42.

10. Ulrich Heimrath, "Hugo von Hofmannsthals 'Reitergeschichte,' " *Wirkendes Wort* 21 (1971) : 315.

11. Alewyn, p. 84.

12. William R. Donlop. "Archetypal Vision in Hofmannsthals's *Reitergeschichte*," *German Life and Letters* 22 (1969) : 131.

13. Hofmannsthal and Schnitzler, p. 280.

14. Fritz Martini, "Hugo von Hofmannsthal: Andreas oder Die Vereinigten," *Hugo von Hofmannsthal*, ed. Sibylle Bauer (Darmstadt, 1968), p. 320.

15. Martini, p. 329.

16. Alewyn, p. 129.

17. See Hugo von Hofmannsthal, "Ein Brief."

18. Herman Broch, "Die Prosaschriften," Bauer, p. 103.

19. Hugo von Hofmannsthal, Notes to *Andreas, oder Die Vereinigten, Gesammelte Werke in Einzelausgaben: Die Erzählungen* (Frankfurt am Main, 1953), p. 203.

20. Hofmannsthal, Notes, p. 204.

21. Manfred Hoppe, *Literatentum, Magie und Mystik im Frühwerk Hugo von Hofmannsthals* (Berlin. 1968). p. 96.

22. Hofmannsthal, Notes, p. 199.

23. Hofmannsthal, Notes, p. 201.

24. Hofmannsthal, Notes, p. 204.

4. LIFE IS A DRAMA

1. Hugo von Hofmannsthal, *Briefe 1890–1901* (Berlin, 1935), p. 185.

2. For comments on *The Tower* as a "drama of the world," see Grete Schaeder, "Hugo von Hofmannsthals Weg zur Tragödie," *Deutsche Vierteljahrsschrift für Literaturwissenschaft und Geistesgeschichte* 23, 2–3 (1949), especially p. 334.

3. Bertolt Brecht, "Hofmannsthals 'Jedermann' im Stadttheater," *Hofmannsthal im Urteil seiner Kritiker*, ed. Gotthart Wunberg (Frankfurt am Main, 1972), p. 288.

4. Hugo von Hofmannsthal and Richard Strauss, *A Working Friendship*, trans. Hanns Hammelmann and Ewald Osers (New York, 1961), p. 182.

5. For a more detailed discussion of the "preexistence" concept, see the chapter "Life Is a Poem."

6. Hanns A. Hammelmann, *Hugo von Hofmannsthal* (London, 1957), pp. 36–37.

7. Hugo von Hofmannsthal, "Briefe an Irene und Paul Hellmann," *Jahrbuch der Deutschen Schiller-Gesellschaft* 11 (1967): 200.

8. Hofmannsthal and Strauss, pp. 357–358.

9. Emil Staiger, "Hugo von Hofmannsthal 'Der Schwierige,'" in *Hugo von Hofmannsthal*, ed. Sibylle Bauer (Darmstadt, 1968), p. 404.

10. Hugo von Hofmannsthal, "Eleonora Duse," *Gesammelte*

Werke in Einzelausgaben. Prosa I (Frankfurt am Main, 1956), p. 67.

11. Wilhelm Emrich, "Hofmannsthals Lustspiel 'Der Schwierige,' " Bauer, p. 437.

5. LIFE IS A GAME

1. Hugo von Hofmannsthal and Harry Graf Kessler, *Briefwechsel 1898–1929* (Frankfurt am Main, 1968), p. 190.
2. Franz Mehring, "Hofmannsthals 'Die Hochzeit der Sobeide' und 'Der Abenteurer und die Sängerin,' " *Hofmannsthal im Urteil seiner Kritiker*, ed. Gotthart Wunberg (Frankfurt am Main, 1972), p. 58.
3. Günther Erken, *Hofmannsthals dramatischer Stil* (Tübingen, 1967), p. 21.
4. Hofmannsthal and Kessler, p. 280.
5. Hofmannsthal and Kessler, p. 294.
6. For a detailed analysis of chess as a stylistic device in Hofmannsthal's works see Erken's chapter entitled "Das Spiel," pp. 13–68, especially pp. 22–23.
7. For a more detailed discussion of *The Difficult Man*, see the chapter "Life Is a Drama."

6. LIFE IS A DREAM

1. Hugo von Hofmannsthal, *Gesammelte Werke in Einzelausgaben. Aufzeichnungen* (Frankfurt am Main, 1959), p. 108.
2. Hugo von Hofmannsthal and Carl J. Burckhardt, *Briefwechsel* (Frankfurt am Main, 1957), p. 161.
3. D. G. H. Schubert, *Ansichten von der Nachtseite der Naturwissenschaft* (Dresden, 1808), pp. 215–217; A. A. Hüphers, *Dagbok öwer en Resa igenom de under Stora Koppar-Bergs Höfdingdöme Lydande Lähn och Dalarne aar 1757* (Wästeraas, 1762), p. 420.
4. Hugo von Hofmannsthal, *Briefe 1900–1909* (Vienna, 1937), p. 155.

5. Rudolf Goldschmit, *Hofmannsthal* (Velber bei Hannover, 1968), p. 21.

6. Hofmannsthal and Burckhardt, p. 70.

7. Hermann Broch, *Hofmannsthal und seine Zeit* (Frankfurt am Main, 1974), p. 108.

7. LIFE IS A POEM

1. "Vorfrühling," *Blätter für die Kunst*, 2 (1892), pp. 43–44. English translation from *The Lyrical Poems of Hugo von Hofmannsthal*, trans. Charles Wharton Stork (New Haven, 1918), p. 25. Translations of all other poems used in this chapter are mine.

2. Hermann Ubell, "Die Blätter für die Kunst," *Hofmannsthal im Urteil seiner Kritiker*, ed. Gotthart Wunberg (Frankfurt am Main, 1972), p. 65.

3. Albrecht Schaeffer, "Hugo von Hofmannsthal," Wunberg, pp. 306–307.

4. "Eigene Sprache," *Die Zukunft*, 7 (1898), p. 66.

5. Josef Hofmiller, "Hofmannsthal," Wunberg, p. 171.

6. "Erlebnis," *Blätter für die Kunst*, 2 (1892), p. 39.

7. "Terzinen I," *Blätter für die Kunst*, 3 (1896), p. 38.

8. "Terzinen II," *Pan*, 1 (1895) Nr. 2, pp. 86–87.

9. "Ghaselen II," *Corona*, 9 (1940) Nr. 6, pp. 657–658.

10. "Terzinen III," *Pan*, 1 (1895) Nr. 2, pp. 87–88.

11. "Des alten Mannes Sehnsucht nach dem Sommer," *Österreichische Rundschau*, 11 (1907), pp. 103–104.

12. "Prolog zu dem Buch 'Anatol'," in: Arthur Schnitzler, *Anatol*, (Berlin, 1893), pp. 4–6.

13. "Zum Gedächtnis des Schauspielers Mitterwurzer," *Wiener Rundschau*, 2 (1898) Nr. 12, pp. 454–455.

14. "Der Jüngling und die Spinne," *Blätter für die Kunst*, 4 (1899), pp. 74–76.

15. "Ein Prolog," in: Hugo von Hofmannsthal, *Gesammelte Werke in Einzelausgaben. Gedichte und lyrische Dramen*, ed. Herbert Steiner (Stockholm, 1946), pp. 122–136.

16. "Wo ich nahe, wo ich lande . . . ," *Pan. Prospekt-Buch* (Leipzig, 1898), p. 101.

17. Stefan George and Hugo von Hofmannsthal, *Briefwech-sel* (Berlin, 1938), p. 119.

8. SYNTHESIS

1. For a detailed discussion of the essay's relationship to Schiller's thought, see Lowell A. Bangerter, *Schiller and Hofmannsthal*. In English with German quotations (Madrid, 1974), pp. 135–146.
2. Hugo von Hofmannsthal, *Briefe 1890–1901* (Berlin, 1935), p. 295.

Bibliography

Publishing data are offered for the first independent publication and for English translations of the work. Some of the shorter works were first published in periodicals. For complete information on other editions, translations into other languages, and sound recordings of the works, please see: Horst Weber, *Hugo von Hofmannsthal Bibliographie.* Berlin and New York: Walter de Gruyter, 1972.

I.   WORKS BY HUGO VON HOFMANNSTHAL

1.   *Imaginative Writings*

Gestern. Vienna: Verlag der Modernen Rundschau, 1891. Drama.

Der Tor und der Tod (Death and the Fool, trans. Max Batt, Boston: R. G. Badger, 1913; trans. John Heard, Jr. in: *The German Classics*, XVII, New York: The German Publication Society, 1914; trans. Elisabeth Walter, Boston: R. G. Badger, 1914; trans. Montrose John Moses in: *Representative One-Act Plays by Continental Authors*, ed. M. J. Moses, Boston: Little and Brown, 1922; The Fool and Death, trans. Herbert Edward Mierow, Colorado Springs: Colorado College Publications, 1930; Death and the Fool, trans. Michael Hamburger in: Hugo von Hofmannsthal, *Selected Writings*, II, New York: Pantheon, 1961; trans. Alfred Schwarz in: Hugo von Hofmannsthal, *Three Plays*, Detroit: Wayne State University Press, 1966). Munich: Knorr und Hirth, 1899. Drama.

Die Hochzeit der Sobeide (The Marriage of Sobeide, trans. Bayard Q. Morgan in: *The German Classics of the*

Nineteenth and Twentieth Centuries, eds. Kuno Francke
and W. G. Howard, New York: German Publishing
Society, 1920; The Marriage of Zobeide, trans. Christo-
pher Middleton in: Hugo von Hofmannsthal, *Poems and
Verse Plays*, New York: Pantheon, 1961). Berlin:
Theater-Verlag A. Entsch, 1899. Drama.

Theater in Versen. Berlin: Fischer, 1899. Drama.

Der Kaiser und die Hexe (The Emperor and the Witch,
trans. Christopher Middleton in: Hugo von Hofmannsthal, *Poems and Verse Plays*, New York: Pantheon,
1961). Leipzig: Insel, 1900. Drama.

Der Schüler. Berlin: Fischer, 1902. Drama.

Ausgewählte Gedichte. Berlin: Verlag der Blätter für die
Kunst, 1903. Poetry.

Das kleine Welttheater (The Little Theater of the World or
the Fortunate Ones, trans. Michael Hamburger in: Hugo
von Hofmannsthal, *Poems and Verse Plays*, New York:
Pantheon, 1961). Leipzig: Insel, 1903. Drama.

Elektra (Electra, trans. Arthur Symons, New York: Bren-
tano's, 1908; also in: *Chief Contemporary Dramatists*,
ed. Thomas H. Dickinson, Cambridge, Massachusetts:
The Riverside Press, 1958; trans. Alfred Schwarz in:
Hugo von Hofmannsthal, *Three Plays*, Detroit: Wayne
State University Press, 1966; trans. Carl Richard Muel-
ler in: Robert W. Corrigan, *Masterpieces of the Modern
Central European Theater*, New York: Collier Books,
1967). Berlin: Fischer, 1904. Drama.

Unterhaltungen über literarische Gegenstände, ed. Georg
Brandes. Berlin: Bard und Marquardt, 1904. Essays.

Das gerettete Venedig (Venice Preserved, trans. Elisabeth
Walter, Boston: R. G. Badger, 1915). Berlin: Fischer,
1905. Drama.

Das Märchen der 672. Nacht, und andere Erzahlungen.
Vienna and Leipzig: Wiener Verlag, 1905. Prose Fiction.

Kleine Dramen. Leipzig: Insel, 1906. Drama.

Oedipus und die Sphinx (Oedipus and the Sphinx, trans.
Gertrude Schoenbohm in: *Oedipus: Myth and Drama*,
eds. Martin Kalich, et al., New York: Odyssey, 1968).
Berlin: Fischer, 1906. Drama.

Der Weisse Fächer (The White Fan, trans. Maurice Magnus

in: *The Mask: The Journal of the Art of the Theater*, Florence, I, Nr. 12, February 1909). Leipzig: Insel, 1907. Drama.

Die Gesammelten Gedichte. Leipzig: Insel, 1907. Poetry.

Die prosaischen Schriften 3 vols. Berlin: Fischer, 1907, 1917. Essays.

Vorspiele. Leipzig: Insel, 1908. Drama.

Der Abenteurer und die Sängerin. Berlin: Fischer, 1909. Drama.

Die Frau im Fenster (Madonna Dianora, trans. Harriet Betty Boas in: *Fifty Contemporary One-Act Plays*, eds. Frank Shay and Pierre Loving, New York: Appleton, 1925). Berlin: Fischer, 1909. Drama.

Cristinas Heimreise (Cristina's Journey Home, trans. Roy Temple House, Boston: R. G. Badger, 1916). Berlin: Fischer, 1910. Drama.

König Oedipus. Berlin: Fischer, 1910. Drama.

Alkestis. Leipzig: Insel, 1911. Drama.

Der Rosenkavalier (The Rose-Bearer, trans. Alfred Kalisch, Berlin and Paris: Adolph Fürstner, 1912; The Cavalier of the Rose, trans. Christopher Holme in: Hugo von Hofmannsthal, *Selected Plays and Libretti*, New York: Pantheon, 1963). Berlin: Fischer, 1911. Libretto.

Jedermann (The Play of Everyman, trans. George Sterling and Richard Ordynski, San Francisco: A. M. Robertson, 1917; trans. Wheeler and Sybil Amherst, Via Crucis, 1923; The Salzburg Everyman, trans. M. E. Tafler, Salzburg: Verlag M. Mora, 1929, 1946). Berlin: Fischer, 1911. Drama.

Ariadne auf Naxos (Ariadne on Naxos, trans. Alfred Kalisch, Berlin: Fürstner, 1922). Berlin and Paris: Fürstner, 1912. Libretto.

Der Bürger als Edelmann. Berlin: Fürstner, 1912. Drama.

Josephslegende (The Legend of Joseph, trans. Alfred Kalisch, Berlin and Paris: Fürstner, 1914). Berlin: Fürstner, 1914. Ballet.

Die Frau ohne Schatten (The Woman without a Shadow, trans. Publicity Dept. Decca Record Co., London: Decca Record Co., 1957). Berlin: Fürstner, 1916. Libretto.

Das Märchen der 672. Nacht (Tale of the Merchant's Son

and His Servants, trans. Alan D. Trethewey in: *The Lion Rampart*, Cambridge, Massachusetts, 1969). Leipzig: Insel, 1918. Prose Fiction.

Dame Kobold. Berlin: Fischer, 1920. Drama.

Die Frau ohne Schatten. Berlin: Fischer, 1920. Prose Fiction.

Reitergeschichte (Cavalry Patrol, trans. Basil Creighton in: *Tellers of Tales*, ed. W. Somerset Maugham, New York: Doubleday, Doran and Co., 1939; Cavalry Tale, trans. E. B. Ashton in: *The Best of Modern European Literature*, eds. Klaus Mann and Hermann Kesten, Philadelphia: Blakiston, 1945; A Tale of the Cavalry, trans. Mary D. Hottinger in: Hugo von Hofmannsthal, *Selected Prose*, New York: Pantheon, 1952). Vienna: Strache, 1920. Prose Fiction.

Der Schwierige (The Difficult Man, trans. Willa Muir in: Hugo von Hofmannsthal, *Selected Plays and Libretti*, New York: Pantheon, 1963). Berlin: Fischer, 1921. Drama.

Reden und Aufsätze. Leipzig: Insel, 1921. Essays.

Das Salzburger große Welttheater (The Salzburg Great Theater of the World, trans. Vernon Watkins in: Hugo von Hofmannsthal, *Selected Plays and Libretti*, New York: Pantheon, 1963). Leipzig: Insel, 1922. Drama.

Die grüne Flöte. Vienna and Leipzig: Universal-Edition, 1923. Ballet.

Florindo. Vienna and Hellerau: Avalun, 1923. Drama.

Prima Ballerina. Vienna and Leipzig: Universal-Edition, 1923. Ballet.

Augenblicke in Griechenland (Moments in Greece, trans. Tania and James Stern in: Hugo von Hofmannsthal, *Selected Prose*, New York: Pantheon, 1952). Regensburg and Leipzig: Habbel & Naumann, 1924. Essays.

Achilles auf Skyros. Vienna and New York: Universal-Edition, 1925. Ballet.

Der Turm (The Tower, trans. Michael Hamburger in: Hugo von Hofmannsthal, *Selected Plays and Libretti*, New York: Pantheon, 1963; trans. Alfred Schwarz in: Hugo von Hofmannsthal, *Three Plays*, Detroit: Wayne State University Press, 1966). Munich: Verlag der Bremer Presse, 1925. (Second Version: Berlin: Fischer, 1927.) Drama.

Die Ruinen von Athen. Berlin: Fürstner, 1925. Ballet.

Früheste Prosastücke. Leipzig: Gesellschaft der Freunde der deutschen Bücherei, 1926. Essays.

Drei Erzählungen. Leipzig: Insel, 1927. Prose Fiction.

Der Tod des Tizian (The Death of Titian, trans. John Heard, Jr., Boston: Four Seas, 1914). Leipzig: Insel, 1928. Drama.

Die ägyptische Helene (Helen in Egypt, trans. Alfred Kalisch, Berlin: Fürstner; New York: Ricordi & Co., 1928). Leipzig: Insel, 1928. Libretto.

Loris. Berlin: Fischer, 1930. Poetry.

Die Berührung der Sphären. Berlin: Fischer, 1931. Essays.

Wege und Begegnungen. Leipzig: Reclam, 1931. Essays.

Andreas, oder Die Vereinigten (Andreas, or The United, trans. Marie D. Hottinger, London: Dent & Sons, 1936; Andreas, trans. Marie D. Hottinger in: Hugo von Hofmannsthal, *Selected Prose*, New York: Pantheon, 1952). Berlin: Fischer, 1932. Prose Fiction.

Das Bergwerk zu Falun (The Mine at Falun, trans. Michael Hamburger in: Hugo von Hofmannsthal, *Poems and Verse Plays*, New York: Pantheon, 1961). Vienna: Wiener Bibliophilen-Gesellschaft, 1933. Drama.

Arabella (Arabella, trans. John Gutman, New York: Boosey & Hawkes, 1955; London: Boosey & Hawkes, 1965; trans. Nora Wydenbruck and Christopher Middleton in: Hugo von Hofmannsthal, *Selected Plays and Libretti*, New York: Pantheon, 1963). Berlin: Fürstner, 1933. Libretto.

Der Unbestechliche. Berlin: Fischer, 1933. Drama.

Nachlese der Gedichte. Berlin: Fischer, 1934. Poetry.

Dramatische Entwürfe. Vienna: Verlag der Johannes-Presse, 1936. Drama.

Das Leben ein Traum. Corona, 7 (1937), pp. 60–93, 269–271. Drama.

Festspiele in Salzburg. Vienna: Bermann-Fischer, 1938. Essays.

Gesammelte Werke in Einzelausgaben, ed. Herbert Steiner, 15 vols. Stockholm: Bermann-Fischer, 1945ff.; Frankfurt on the Main: Fischer, 1950ff. Collected Works.

Erlebnis des Marschalls von Bassompierre und andere Er-

zählungen. Zurich: Verlag der Arche, 1950. Prose Fiction.

Sylvia im "Stern," ed. Martin Stern. Bern and Stuttgart: Paul Haupt, 1959. Drama.

Das erzählerische Werk. Frankfurt on the Main: Fischer, 1969. Prose Fiction.

Reitergeschichte: Erzählungen und Aufsätze. Frankfurt on the Main: Fischer, 1969. Prose Fiction and Essays.

2. *Correspondence and Diaries*

Buch der Freunde. Leipzig: Insel, 1922.

Briefe 1890–1901. Berlin: Fischer, 1935.

Der Briefwechsel Hofmannsthal-Wildgans, ed. Joseph A. von Bradisch. Zurich, Munich, Paris: Franklin Press, 1935.

Briefe 1900–1909. Vienna: Bermann-Fischer, 1937.

Briefwechsel zwischen George und Hofmannsthal, ed. Robert Boehringer. Berlin: Bondi, 1938.

Strauss, Richard and Hugo von Hofmannsthal. *Briefwechsel* (Correspondence between Richard Strauss and Hugo von Hofmannsthal, trans. Paul England, New York: Alfred A. Knopf; London: Martin Secker, 1927; A Working Friendship, trans. Hanns Hammelmann and Ewald Osers, New York: Random House; London: Collins, 1961), eds. Franz and Alice Strauss. Zurich: Atlantis, 1952.

Hofmannsthal, Hugo von and Eberhard von Bodenhausen. *Briefe der Freundschaft,* ed. Dora von Bodenhausen. Berlin: Eugen Diederichs, 1953.

Hofmannsthal, Hugo von and Rudolf Borchardt. *Briefwechsel,* eds. Marie Luise Borchardt and Herbert Steiner. Frankfurt on the Main: Fischer, 1954.

Hofmannsthal, Hugo von and Carl J. Burckhardt. *Briefwechsel,* ed. Carl J. Burckhart. Frankfurt on the Main: Fischer, 1956.

Gesammelte Werke in Einzelausgaben: Aufzeichnungen, ed. Herbert Steiner. Frankfurt on the Main: Fischer, 1959.

"Briefe an Willy Wiegand und die Bremer Presse," ed. Werner Volke. *Jahrbuch der Deutschen Schiller-Gesellschaft,* 7 (1963), pp. 44–189.

Hofmannsthal, Hugo von and Arthur Schnitzler. *Briefwechsel*, eds. Therese Nickl and Heinrich Schnitzler. Frankfurt on the Main: Fischer, 1964.

Hofmannsthal, Hugo von and Helene von Nostitz-Wallwitz. *Briefwechsel*, ed. Oswalt von Nostitz. Frankfurt on the Main: Fischer, 1965.

Hofmannsthal, Hugo von and Edgar Karg von Bebenburg. *Briefwechsel*, ed. Mary E. Gilbert. Frankfurt on the Main: Fischer, 1966.

Briefe an Marie Herzfeld, ed. Horst Weber. Heidelberg: Stiehm, 1967.

"Briefe an Irene und Paul Hellmann," ed. Werner Volke. *Jahrbuch der Deutschen Schiller-Gesellschaft*, 11 (1967), pp. 170–224.

Hofmannsthal, Hugo von and Leopold von Andrian. *Briefwechsel*, ed. Walter Perl. Frankfurt on the Main: Fischer, 1968.

Hofmannsthal, Hugo von and Willy Haas. *Ein Briefwechsel*, ed. Willy Haas. Berlin: Propyläen, 1968.

Hofmannsthal, Hugo von and Harry Graf Kessler. *Briefwechsel 1898–1929*, ed. Hilde Burger. Frankfurt on the Main: Insel, 1968.

Hofmannsthal, Hugo von and Josef Redlich. *Briefwechsel*, ed. Helga Fussgänger. Frankfurt on the Main: Fischer, 1971.

Hofmannsthal, Hugo von and Richard Beer-Hoffmann. *Briefwechsel*, ed. Eugene Weber. Frankfurt on the Main: Fischer, 1972.

Hofmannsthal, Hugo von and Ottonie von Degenfeld. *Briefwechsel*, ed. Marie Therese Miller-Degenfeld. Frankfurt on the Main: Fischer, 1974.

3. *Works Edited by Hofmannsthal*

Deutsche Erzähler 4 vols. Leipzig: Insel, 1912.

Österreichischer Almanach auf das Jahr 1916, Leipzig: Insel, 1916.

Deutsches Lesebuch 2 vols. Munich: Bremer Presse, 1922f.

Deutsche Epigramme. Munich: Bremer Presse, 1923.

Schillers Selbstcharakteristik. Munich: Bremer Presse, 1926.

Wert und Ehre deutscher Sprache. Munich: Bremer Presse, 1927.

4. *Collected Works in English Translation*

The Lyrical Poems of Hugo von Hofmannsthal, trans. Charles Wharton Stork. New Haven: Yale University Press, 1918.

Selected Prose, trans. Mary Hottinger and Tania and James Stern. New York: Pantheon, 1952.

Poems and Verse Plays, ed. Michael Hamburger. New York: Pantheon, 1961.

Selected Plays and Libretti, ed. Michael Hamburger. New York: Pantheon, 1963.

Three Plays, trans. Alfred Schwarz. Detroit: Wayne State University Press, 1966.

II. WORKS ABOUT HOFMANNSTHAL

Alewyn, Richard. *Über Hugo von Hofmannsthal*. Göttingen: Vandenhoeck und Ruprecht, 1967.

Bangerter, Lowell A. *Schiller and Hofmannsthal*. Madrid: Dos Continentes, 1974.

Bauer, Sibylle, ed. *Hugo von Hofmannsthal*. Darmstadt: Wissenschaftliche Buchgesellschaft, 1968.

Broch, Hermann. *Hofmannsthal und seine Zeit*. Frankfurt am Main: Suhrkamp, 1974.

Burckhardt, Carl J. *Erinnerungen an Hofmannsthal*. Munich: Callwey, 1964.

Coghlan, Brian L. *Hofmannsthal's Festival Dramas*. Cambridge: Cambridge University Press, 1964.

Erken, Günther. *Hofmannsthals dramatischer Stil*. Tübingen: Niemeyer, 1967.

Esselborn, Karl G. *Hofmannsthal und der antike Mythos*. Munich: Fink, 1969.

Fiechtner, Helmut A., ed. *Hugo von Hofmannsthal*. Bern and Munich: Francke, 1963.

Gerke, Ernst-Otto. *Der Essay als Kunstform bei Hugo von Hofmannsthal*. Lübeck: Matthiesen, 1970.

Goldschmit, Rudolf. *Hofmannsthal.* Velber bei Hannover: Friedrich, 1968.

Hammelmann, Hanns A. *Hugo von Hofmannsthal.* London: Bowes and Bowes, 1957.

Hederer, Edgar. *Hugo von Hofmannsthal.* Frankfurt am Main: Fischer, 1960.

Hoppe, Manfred. *Literantentum, Magie und Mystik im Frühwerk Hugo von Hofmannsthals.* Berlin: DeGruyter, 1968.

Kobel, Erwin. *Hugo von Hofmannsthal.* Berlin: DeGruyter, 1970.

Köhler, Wolfgang. *Hugo von Hofmannsthal und "Tausendundeine Nacht."* Bern and Frankfurt am Main: Lang, 1972.

Laubach, Jakob. *Hugo von Hofmannsthals Turmdichtungen.* Kempten: Kösel, 1954.

Naef, Karl J. *Hugo von Hofmannsthals Wesen und Werk.* Leipzig: Mehans, 1938.

Norman, F., ed. *Hofmannsthal.* London: London Institute of Germanic Studies, 1963.

Pickerodt, Gerhart. *Hofmannsthals Dramen.* Stuttgart: Metzler, 1968.

Pulver, Elsbeth. *Hofmannsthals Schriften zur Literatur.* Bern: Paul Haupt, 1956.

Ritter, Frederick. *Hugo von Hofmannsthal und Österreich.* Heidelberg: Stiehm, 1967.

Schaeder, Grete. *Hugo von Hofmannsthal.* Berlin: Junker und Dünnhaupt, 1933.

Weber, Horst. *Hugo von Hofmannsthal. Bibliographie des Schrifttums* 1892–1963. Berlin: DeGruyter, 1966.

Wunberg, Gotthart. *Der frühe Hofmannsthal.* Stuttgart, Berlin, Cologne, Mainz: Kohlhammer, 1965.

Wunberg, Gotthart, ed. *Hofmannsthal im Urteil seiner Kritiker.* Frankfurt am Main: Athenäum, 1972.

Index

MODERN LITERATURE MONOGRAPHS

In the same series (*continued from page ii*)